S.O.A.P.
FRA

Identifying, Diagnosing, and Curing those Nagging Business Problems

DR. BERNARD GRAMLICH

San Diego

Contents

Copyright	iii
Dedication	iv
Introduction	v
Chapter 1	1
Building a Framework Against Failure	
Chapter 2	8
Lessons from My Past	
Chapter 3	25
The SOAP Framework	
Chapter 4	38
The Active Business Plan	
Chapter 5	55
Marketing Strategies with S.O.A.P.	
Chapter 6	72
Business Strategies Using S.O.A.P.	
Chapter 7	87
Building Relationships with Vendors	
Chapter 8	103
Tracking Numbers	
Chapter 9	123
Improving the Sales Process with S.O.A.P.	
Chapter 10	146
Daily Focus Techniques	
Chapter 11	154
Conclusion	
About The Author	163

COPYRIGHT

S.O.A.P. Framework
© 2015 by Dr. Bernard Gramlich

All rights reserved. No part of this publication may be reproduced, stored in a retrieval system, or transmitted by any means – electronic, mechanical, photographic (photocopying), recording, or otherwise – without prior permission in writing from the author.

Limit of Liability/Disclaimer of Warranty: While the publisher and author have used their best efforts in preparing this book, they make no representations or warranties with respect to the accuracy or completeness of the contents of this book and specifically disclaim any implied warranties of merchantability or fitness for a particular purpose. No warranty may be created or extended by sales representatives or written sales materials. The advice and strategies contained herein may not be suitable for your situation. You should consult with a professional where appropriate. Neither the publisher nor author shall be liable for any loss of profit or any other commercial damages, including but not limited to special, incidental, consequential, or other damages.

Printed in the United States of America

Learn more information at: drgramconsulting.com

ISBN 978-0-692-38259-2 e-book

ISBN 978-1508484127 Paperback

Dedication

Dedicated to my wife Marisol, and my awesome boys Liam and Bryce, who have been by my side for this crazy ride (and giving me unwavering support every step of the way). I love each of you with all my heart.

Introduction

The biggest problem facing most entrepreneurs and business owners today is a lack of *focus*. There are so many moving parts to a business that we often lose our focus and start dropping the ball on key elements. Between balancing a family, managing employees and customers, maintaining social contact on Facebook and Twitter and dealing with the *fear of failure*, it's no wonder eight out of 10 businesses never succeed. We need better tools to help us focus on solving the issues, problems and challenges we face on a daily basis.

As an entrepreneur, I was very unhappy with my corporate job. I did not like selling products that were inferior and I absolutely hated the way I was asked to treat customers as numbers. There was no service aspect at all. There is a strong chance you know exactly what I'm talking about and have experienced similar feelings in your old corporate job which is why you also chose to start your own business. Then, after starting your own business, you discovered it was a lot harder than you ever expected. Trust me. I felt the same way. Every little problem feels like a catastrophe, but then something somewhere pulls you back in and you go back to fight another day. Something can *and will* go wrong every day, and what is going to define you as a true entrepreneur is how quickly you get it solved and move on to the important parts of business, like growing it and providing great service.

I started my mornings out the same way every day when I opened my first pharmacy. This helped me get the focus I would need for the day and got me pumped up so I could walk in the door and start tackling the issues on my to-do list and start thinking about reaching the next milestone in my professional life. I listened to Eminem's song "Lose Yourself." The line in the song that stuck with me and motivated me was, "Success is my only *"bad word"* option, failure's not."

I am not sure why, but that line from the song was able to get me to focus on the task at hand when I walked through the door at work. The determination that he has in the song to do what he loved, provide for his family and give other people pleasure with his music gave me the energy to get in my office and kick butt. The hard part is keeping that feeling going throughout the day when issues and problems are killing your productivity. That song was the short burst of motivation and I needed something that would carry me for the life of my business. I needed a model that would help maintain focus on the ultimate goal of viability.

One of my biggest obstacles I faced was my own pride. I felt that if I asked for help from my friends or family, they would laugh at me. I felt they would say, "He opened a business and can't solve some of the simplest problems." Now, I know it was not pride; it was fear and lack of focus. After starting your business, you are filled with excitement and fear, but the fear always seems to have a stronger hold. I started to break that once I realized that fear is a type of focus and you can turn that negative into a positive with just a little help. The two things that helped me turn my business into a profitable and viable business in less than ten months was getting advice from my mentors and building the repeatable framework to solve the issues and challenges I had in my business.

I call it the S.O.A.P. Framework. The S.O.A.P. Framework helped me convert my fear into the focus that grew the business from negative revenue to in excess of a million a year. At the end of nine years, I was doing

9 million a year in revenue. The S.O.A.P. Framework is an easy tool that you can use to streamline processes in your business to reach efficiency and profitability. That way you can start to focus on the growth of your business to get it to a viable state, which is the goal of every entrepreneur.

   I struggled for years because I would try to figure everything out on my own. When I did look for help, I had problems picking the right tools for the right situations. Then one day, a patient came in to the pharmacy to get advice about her cancer treatments. I went through my normal questioning process to get the answers I needed to help her with her problem. After she left, I started to ask myself, "if I can use the technique I learned in school to answer questions and help solve a problem that a cancer patient has, then why can't I use those same techniques to solve my business woes?" This is when I started to develop my framework. Once I created the S.O.A.P. Framework, my focused changed and the business started to grow in ways I hadn't expected. I experienced a growth in my sales, my confidence, and the business's honest reputation which piqued my interest in an expansion. At first, I just wanted to grab more of the market share in San Diego. However, with a little push from my friend Jason, I

Introduction

opened a new store. The crazy part is that not only was I opening a new store, I was doing it in Henderson, NV. I guess stress was a great motivator for me. After sitting down with my future pharmacy manager Jason, the same one that talked me into expanding, we began discussing the business model and plan that I built for the pharmacy in San Diego. We both had the confidence that this pharmacy was going to be successful. The goal was to build a business that people would love to come to for the great service and compassion. The medications and other healthcare products are the same at every other store, but the value in our service and compassion is what helped that business become a viable business in less than one year. Now, don't get me wrong. I was nervous and there was some fear, but it was quickly converted to pure focus because I knew I could lean on my framework to get out of a jam, if needed.

In this book, I will go over some strategies for business growth and you will learn the S.O.A.P. Framework. With the S.O.A.P. Framework, you will learn how to focus your efforts on the challenges that come up during the daily course of the business. It will also give you the confidence to operate without fear and help keep the focus you will need to grow a viable business. I will cover a variety of business-related experiences that I have had personally and some with my clients over the years and how the S.O.A.P. Framework can save time and money. I will talk about the importance of having a business plan. Some of the other chapters will cover marketing, sales, operations and vendors. The S.O.A.P. Framework will help you stay focused to perform at a high level in your business. Your business will run at a greater efficiency and profitability, which leads to success, and legacy.

Over the years, I have gradually perfected the S.O.A.P. Framework to make it easy to use. My clients have had great success utilizing the framework in their day-to-day operations to reach better profitability while working fewer hours so they can enjoy their life, business and family.

Chapter 1

Building a Framework Against Failure

The current viewpoint of entrepreneur-owned businesses is in a state of confusion. In a recent business survey from March of 2013, 43 percent of the businesses felt that we were in a recession. 45 percent felt that we were in a recovery phase. Only 1 percent said that business was in an expansion phase. This just goes to show you that the business world is equally confused about the country's financial health. However, the one constant was that every business surveyed in the U.S. felt that higher taxes and regulations were to blame for failing businesses. I disagree with some of that because businesses don't fail – the entrepreneur fails, and that leads to the closing of doors. Changing your focus and anticipating the future of your business will help your success rate climb. Being able to meet challenges before they become problems is a key attribute to business success. The challenges are sometimes overwhelming, and if you don't have the tools and mindset in place, failure will be staring you in the face. Walking through the doors of your business on the first day is often filled with optimism and excitement because up to this point all you have had to do is find a location, some furniture and go to Staples for some office supplies. But, on the first day when the doors open and your first customer walks in and you cannot deliver on your advertising promises, this will scare the crap out of you. This is when all of the doubts creep in and Nay Sayers seem to come out of the woodwork to haunt you. I feel that these are some of the biggest reasons that businesses fail in the first one to five years.

We have all heard the statistic that 55 percent of businesses fail within the first five years. On the other hand, to boost your spirits a bit, there are plenty of statistics that show when the economy is in the toilet, start-up businesses begin to pop up and make the economy stronger. There are plenty of entrepreneurs who say screw the big box companies and we will make our own jobs. We start looking for openings in the marketplace for a product and service and fill

CHAPTER 1

it with our own great product or service.

   A different approach is needed when you open the doors to your new business. Take a step back and look differently at your inventory management and cut out the middleman. This will help save your company tons of money by dealing directly with the suppliers for your business needs. Listening to your clients is another focus you can use in your business. Your clients are the best R&D department you will ever need. So, use them! An exciting thing that I focused on was making the work place a bit more exciting for the staff. If the work place is a fun place, then the employees are more productive and the customers see it and it will build loyalty.

   Now, for some bad news. If you continue to do the same old thing and not review the systems that you have in place, then you are leading your business down a dangerous path to failure. New business owners that leave big box corporations and try to run their businesses the same way are in trouble. Small businesses can not and should not run their businesses like the big corporations. Why? Because as a small business owner we have the ability to make a quicker pivot and change the direction of the business where the larger businesses can not make that kind of move without interference from the board, legal or a stuffy manager getting in the way. My advice is to use the tools you learned and mold them into a model that works for your clients. Notice I did not say works for you! Servicing your clients' needs becomes your primary concern. You will not have to reinvent the wheel, but you will have to do some serious soul searching and look at the business with a keen eye to see where you can be better than your competition while catering to your market.

Your new approach to running a business is going to force you to step outside your comfort zone and look at new options. It's important to have a clear focus and the right tools at your disposal to work for you and not against you. Besides changing what your business does by utilizing the resources available to you like the SBA, SCORE, and the S.O.A.P. Framework, these will help build better systems and increase the clarity the business will need to make it past that ugly five year mark. The last thing that you want to be is a statistic in the U.S. Census Bureau.

The ones that are successful are the ones that look at each system in their business and review it for more effective and efficient ways of doing each task. Go back and dig out the business plan and look to see where you are now and compare it to where you thought you would be at this same time. Take the time to review the sales process and see where it can be streamlined and make sure that the marketing and sales processes are in line with each other. I've never understood why businesses try to keep the production, sales and marketing people in different rooms. They should be working together, not against each other.

The ones that lose are the business owners that don't take advantage of the new technologies and tools like the S.O.A.P. Framework to increase their revenues and profitability by reviewing the business procedures and solving their frustrating problems. It is much better to turn these into opportunities so they can achieve liberation and success in their entrepreneurial world.

When I was faced with business challenges in the beginning of my career, I was the "do it myself guy", but that strategy did not help me reach the goals I set for my business and myself. I was able to reach a level of success because of hard work. Yet, if I would have had a better framework or reached out for professional help from mentors or consultants, I could have reached my goals much faster.

This is the point where I took a couple of steps back and looked for a better way. I pulled all my resources together that I had and I contacted my mentor. After that meeting I was on a warpath to solve the business challenges I was facing. I had many systems that were not working at peak efficiency and my sales were not growing fast enough. In the past, one of my strong points was using my skills to solve problems. Yet, I wasn't doing that. Being caught up in the day to day business activities, you tend to forget your strengths sometimes. My next step was to start reviewing the systems I had and breaking them down to see where I could improve them. This is where I started to refine my S.O.A.P. Framework. Over the years of applying the S.O.A.P. Framework and refining the process, the businesses began to run efficiently, effectively and profitably. The S.O.A.P. Framework gave me the opportunity to work *ON* my business and not *IN* my business.

While building the S.O.A.P. Framework, I had wanted it to be able to work in different industries because of all the different kinds of businesses that I have owned. The other piece of the puzzle was to make it simple enough to where the staff could use it to solve problems or challenges in their departments.

Chapter 1 | Building a Framework Against Failure

 One of the biggest revelations I have had as a business owner is in my philosophy to get started off on the right foot and hit the ground running. Don't be afraid to ask for help and arm yourself with the tools that will move your company from start-up phase to a self-sustaining viable business. Strive for one that provides a product or service that helps makes your customers lives easier., gives the employees a place that they are proud to call work and support, and one that supports the goals and dreams you have for business and family.

 Things have changed in the world of business and the S.O.A.P. Framework will bring peace of mind to the most skilled entrepreneur when it comes to solving the challenges that he or she faces in their business today. The S.O.A.P. Framework has helped grow my first pharmacy from almost nothing to a viable ten million dollar a year business. I am super confident that by following my framework, it will help support your efforts in building a better business and give you the focus you will need to be a more successful entrepreneur.

CHAPTER 2

Lessons from My Past

Waking up to a wet and rainy day in southern Georgia, I remember it was a Wednesday morning way back when I was ten years old. I walked out in to the living room and saw my mother opening and sorting Amway products that she sold to her clients. At that time, Amway was a home based business that sold laundry detergent, a few other household cleaners and supplements. Our neighbor Jim Lewis introduced the business to my mother who was recently divorced and had no work experience. Soon after mom started with Amway, she was frustrated and she quickly knew that being an entrepreneur was not for her.

I asked my mom and Jim to meet and I asked if I could help run the sales and deliveries of the products. Mom was excited that I was interested and Jim was intrigued to see how the meeting would go with a 10 year old leading them. Jim coached me on the meeting and soon I was off and running. Since we lived in a small town outside of Atlanta, I was able to drive the tractor to deliver the products to our clients. That was the best part!

While spending time with Jim to learn the business side of Amway and giving presentations to potential new clients, this is where the juices started to flow to become a lifelong entrepreneur. This was the foundation of my business career.

Now, at ten, I lacked focus and knowledge about business, yet the lessons that excited me the most were sales and marketing. I also really enjoyed the challenge of getting people to listen to a young boy to buy products. This pushed just the right button in me to want to learn more about business.

After a few years of Amway, I wanted to expand my horizon in the business world so at the age of sixteen I went from job to job trying to figure out what I really wanted to do. My mother was upset with me because she felt I could not hold a job, but that was not the case at all. I just wanted to learn as many industries as I could because I knew it would make me a better businessman one day. I worked in factories, restaurants and gyms. I sold products and services, and the list goes on. The best part was that each new job taught me a new skill, and I was bound and determined to mold those skills into a career.

The part of every job that I loved was problem solving. Most of my managers would call on me when something was not working right or there was some type of dispute. I was bold and asked the questions to get right to the pain of the problem. To me, this was awesome because my managers would start to trust me with bigger, more complex problems. When their bosses asked them where and how they came up with the plan, they would say that I helped, and this pushed my status as the problem solver. To me, solving problems was exciting.

I had a knack to handle problems with effective and efficient solutions and I owe this debt of gratitude to my previous employers. They gave me this opportunity to mold and grow my problem solving skills so I could be the entrepreneur I am today.

Finally, at the age of 30, I woke up in my apartment in Los Angeles and realized that I could not live like this anymore. I was tired of going from job to job and not really having a focus on life, career, family, or really anything except for learning. One of the reasons I made some changes and started to settle down into a career was my sister Jeanne. Jeanne sat me down and told me that I couldn't be a nomad anymore. She told me that she hated me for not getting my life together and that I was wasting my talent. At first I did not get what she meant. Then, that morning, August 10th, I woke up in a cold sweat and suddenly it hit me like a ton of bricks.

    I had to stop learning a little bit here and there and start putting my skills into action. Be a doer, not a talker! Later that afternoon I sat down and wrote out my life plan. My life plan included completing my education, treating my family with more respect and getting myself into a career where I could make a difference in people's lives. After a few days of soul searching, I set my sights on the first goal which was to complete school. I enrolled at the University of Southern California and signed up for my first classes in my major which was biology with a minor in business. While in college I had to work and the best jobs that fit into my schedule were a waiter and a bartender. Being a bartender was awesome because the bar created an audience for me. I asked every businessman and woman to tell me about their job and why they did it. This way I could learn from them and not change jobs. If I were smarter, I would have written a book about that years ago because I learned some brilliant information. But, I did not have the discipline or focus in the beginning of my life that I have now.

As I plodded through school and learned from my bartending customers, I still did not have a clear view of my end goal in life or business. My plan was changing all the time and I knew I had to settle down and focus on one thing until I mastered it before I could move on to something else. I remember an interview with Kenny Rogers, and he said that it takes ten years to become successful and master a craft. So, then, I built my ten-year plan. Goal number one was to finish school.

Once I got my degree in biology, the question became, "Now what?" I had to remember to take a minute to pat myself on the back because I just finished my first huge goal. Now it was time was to figure out goal number two. I knew where I wanted to go. I just did not know what I wanted to do with my career. After taking a couple of days to put the next phase of my life together, I started to remember how much fun I had selling, marketing and being an entrepreneur. So, I thought to myself, *"Let's do that"*. Since I had just graduated with a degree in Biology, I had to figure out how to apply that to business. As the wheels were turning, an out of the blue opportunity popped up to open an ice cream store. So, I jumped on it!

My first experience as an entrepreneur was opening an ice cream shop with a friend in North Hollywood, California. We jumped into this without a great plan, but with some great ideas. I wanted to make my sister proud and show her that I was a doer not a talker.

Now, the problem with moving too fast is that problems pop up faster than you can solve them. Our problems started in this venture on day one and lasted until the day I sold my half of the business to my partner. The biggest mistake was not having a business plan, marketing plan, an operations plan or any plan except to go out, get business and sell, sell, sell! Even though we had no plan, we started out on fire because we fell into roles that worked. I would go out and sell and get new clients, and my partner would work in the store running the day-to-day operations. He was very good at being an employee, but he did not have the foresight to see the changing climate of the business and make changes to accommodate the growth fast enough. For me, not being in the business daily and seeing how things were being run was the beginning of the end. I was under the impression that he was a good operations guy, and because we never really had any serious discussions about our expertise, the business slowly started to fall apart. I blame myself because I was so focused on selling and getting new business that I did not see our weaknesses until it was too late.

On the upside, I was selling and marketing the business to every person, place and thing in Los Angeles, and within a few short months we were bringing in $15,000 to $20,000 a month selling ice cream, coffee and bagels. Besides the walk-in customers, I went out and got the movie studios to hire us to sell them coffee and bagels in the morning and ice cream for the afternoons as a boost to the bottom line. The problem was that we were growing so fast that we did not have the infrastructure or the finances to handle the growth. We were set up for the grassroots growth pattern, not the speedway growth pattern.

As the revenues grew, we both loved the increase in business, but more problems started to pop up. One problem that jumped up first was hiring new staff. This was a problem because we did not have hiring protocols. If we had a system for hiring, then the new employees would have been properly trained on inventory and other basic operations. The best part about hiring new employees is that it forced us to make a training guide and start to build the policies and procedures for every system in and out of the store. This was the beginning of building a great business foundation. The bad part is that we did not work on this task as a team, so the systems were disjointed which lead to even more breakdowns in the business. I feel the biggest reason they were breaking down is because our communication was horrible. Ask Ben and Jerry. Communication in a partnership is key!

   Unfortunately, after a year of crappy communication and not really working together to solve the problems of the business, we got frustrated with each other, and I sold my part of the business to him. The saddest part of this whole story is that four months after I got out, he completely lost control of the company, and it went belly up.

   Now that the ice cream store was gone, I decided to go back to school and use my biology degree for something, so I got my doctoral degree in pharmacy. While in pharmacy school a friend of mine named Armen who was a pharmacy manager at

Rite Aid convinced me to come and do an internship with him. This turned out to be another stone in the foundation of my career. Rite Aid would send Armen to different stores that were not performing well to increase customer satisfaction and profits. He was considered the "cleanup guy". He would request that I come along, too. During my time there, we cleaned up three stores, and this was better than any college class. This was Problem Solving 101 by fire and brimstone.

When I started my pharmacy internship rotations, I left the Los Angeles area and I moved to San Diego. I had the same mindset to go to troubled stores and help clean them up. I planted the seed in my new manager's head every chance I got, and it slowly helped to build my reputation while in San Diego. After graduation, Rite Aid gave me a chance to show off my talents and start fixing stores on my own. My first store was in Coronado, California, and it was here where I started to hone the skills of problem solving. I just jumped in and worked my butt off cleaning up that store. Within four months, I organized the workflow to increase efficiency and decrease labor hours. I also was able to build the broken reputation from the last pharmacist and start to grow the script count. I felt awesome that it only took me four short months to take a store that was struggling for over a year and bring it back to life. My first mindset was to do whatever needed to be done to make the numbers look good. Looking back at this method, I am happy that I changed my mindset. I took a step back and looked at what the customers were seeing and that is where I started. Most of the changes I made were without the Pharmacy District Managers consent and I am surprised I did not get fired. Not because of the results or because I did something illegal, but because of the manner in which I got the results. Even though I had better customer satisfaction, increased script counts and high margins, I was not fixing all the underlying problems. I fixed all the problems I knew how to fix, but my downfall was not digging deeper to get to the root cause. I was able to get that store running smoothly and profitable and for me the learning experience was priceless.

After a short four months in Coronado, I asked to be transferred to a busier store. You know the old saying, *be careful what you wish for because you might just get it*? Well, I did! They gave me the Del Mar store which was one of the busiest stores they had in California. Again, I was able to get great results and clean the store up. I tweaked my thought process and dug deeper to make sure the root causes of the problems were addressed so when I turned the store over, the next manager only had to run it status quo.

Less than one year at the Del Mar store, I went to Los Angeles to visit my friend Armen. He had moved on from Rite Aid and opened up his own independent pharmacy. Armen is one of those guys that turned everything he touches into platinum. Needless to say, he was and is very successful. We were sitting in his office catching up when a staff member came in to grab him to solve a dispute in the front end. While he was gone I took a quick peep at his QuickBooks. I knew that he was doing well, but I was shocked when I saw how *well* he was doing. This motivated me to leave the corporate world and move on to being an entrepreneur again. Using the education from Rite Aid, I felt I had all the tools to start my own place and forge forward with my entrepreneurial skills to get to the next goal on my life plan: owning and running my own business. I wanted to make it into a viable business which would be bigger, better and faster than any of my friends' businesses.

In January of 2003, I opened Cedar Pharmacy. I was pumped and excited to have my own place. I opened it on credit cards, a prayer and hope. I sat down and wrote out my business plan. I did not want to make the same mistake I made with the ice cream store. Lesson number one for entrepreneurs: *You will make mistakes. Just don't make the same one twice.* Armed with my business plan, skills from Rite Aid and years of learning and mentorship, I was sure that I was going to knock it out of the ballpark in no time.

I went from a busy corporate store that had 15 employees, filling 600 prescriptions a day and tons of problems to solve to a store that had zero employees, filling five prescriptions a day and virtually no problems to really worry about. It felt like I could take a month to solve an issue because there was no real urgency. If there is one thing I have learned about myself over the years, it is that I need to be busy! If I have any down time, I get bored and I look for something to occupy my mind. After two months into the business, I was bored to death and I started thinking, *"What is wrong with these people? They have a pharmacy in the building where their medical doctor is, and there is virtually no wait for their prescriptions. Why are they not coming in?"* This is where I realized I was wrong about taking so much time to solve problems. I had plenty of them and now I needed to use my street MBA, and my business Darwin instincts to grow the business.

I went back and looked at my business plan to make it into a working document. I did this to stop *hoping* people would come in the pharmacy and actually bring them into the pharmacy. I had to go out to get the business. I had two pieces of the puzzle to figure out: what made me different than the chain stores, and why would someone want to leave their current pharmacy and shop at mine? People do not like change. It's human nature to stick with what is comfortable. But, how was I going to get them to overcome their fear and change to my pharmacy? I was sitting on my ass thinking I had no problems and, in reality, I had plenty of problems that needed to be solved ASAP or I would be cashless and homeless.

The same day I came to the revelation that I needed to change my focus at work, I got another surprise when I got home that day. At this point, I got a real kick in the teeth. I had all of my focus on the business and none on my family. I was 5 months into opening my pharmacy and I walked in the house after a long 18-hour day expecting to get a hug and kiss from Marisol, my wife, and hold my newborn son, Liam, but that is not what I got. She was sitting on the couch with Liam and they both were crying. Naturally, being the kind loving husband I thought I was being, I went over and sat down to comfort her and Liam. She pushed me away and asked me, "What was the most important thing to me?" I said that she and the baby were my first priority and that is why I am working so hard to provide for them. She told me that she appreciated the hard work I was doing, but what she really needed was for me to be home to help and be a better father to our son. What I needed to do was to change my focus from business only to a more balanced life. She told me that she loved the fact that I was willing to sacrifice one thing to improve another, but I needed to learn balance to have a better life. The next thing she told me was that if I can't be home to support her and our newborn son, then she would divorce me and move back home with her family to get help. I was thinking, "I just opened a pharmacy and I am struggling to keep it afloat to pay for everything that we have, so why does she not appreciate that?" Like many men, I was only thinking about what I do instead of the stress and pressure my wife was under all day, every day, while raising kids, working and keeping up with the house schedule. I knew that I had to do something to change not only for my marriage, but also for my son. After taking this news hard, I sat back and started to think about what I needed to do better and why.

For me, the 'why' part was easy. I wanted to keep my marriage in place and I really needed to be a better father to my son. The one thing I always promised myself is that I would be a better father to my kids than my father was to his kids. Plus, I was missing key moments in Liam's life that I would never get back. That time was gone forever! Out of all the things we do in this world, we can get everything back except time. Once it's gone, it's gone! In my plan to change the focus about my business, I had to figure out a way to save time so I could make it up to my family. The last thing you want in your life is to look back and say "what if?"

    I put my thinking cap on and started to place more elements in my plan. The problems I had to address were: *Where do I get business? How do I market to them?* What kind of products should I carry to draw the customers in? *What kind of deals can I make as a small fry to the vendors to get good pricing to be competitive in the market place? What kind of value can I provide so I am not viewed as a commodity? How can I make my business more efficient so I can significantly increase my profits while working fewer hours so I can enjoy my life, business and family?* Now that I had all this work to do, I had to focus and get some clarity in the plan to succeed. I had to come up with a plan to get my pharmacy from negative numbers to positive numbers. I had to have a plan for success and, most importantly, I had to visualize it. That is when I really put my nose to the grindstone and developed what is now known as the S.O.A.P. Framework. The S.O.A.P. Framework helped me get my first pharmacy from a red -$18,354 hole per month to a positive $55,668 a month in revenue. By creating a way to focus on every piece of my business and putting the pieces together to have a whole business operating in sequence was an awesome feeling. I was able to work three days a week while making great money and providing a great product and service for the customers while still enjoying my family life. From my second year in business to the day I sold the pharmacy, my focus was on my family, the value I provided, the customers, growing sales and improving my gross margins to the twenty percent range. By focusing on the higher gross margin, the revenues grew between $700k and 1 million dollars per year. The S.O.A.P. Framework enabled me to start working on the business and not in the business. This strategy helped me grow from one pharmacy to four, saved my marriage and allowed me to actively raise my two awesome boys. My sons Liam and Bryce are the fuel that keeps me excited about teaching and growing business. In the next chapter, I will talk about what the S.O.A.P. Framework is and how it works. Then, in the following chapters, I will discuss S.O.A.P. Framework in all the different areas of business, so you will be able to use it to help evaluate each level of your business and use it to improve some of the key elements that make your business thrive.

Chapter 3

The SOAP Framework

As an entrepreneur, the one thing we want is to make a difference in the lives of our customers and employees with a product or service that we care about. Besides your own expectations that you have for yourself, the pressure to perform is greater once you have customers and employees. Having this mindset, my sole focus was making the business viable. Having a viable business meant that I could walk in the office on a daily basis and feel confident that the people I served and my employees could feel safe that they were going to have a place to work every day and earn a living.

Now, I was five months in and Cedar Pharmacy was not looking good. It was June of 2003 and I got to my office, sat down, and put my thinking cap on. I knew that I had to change the way I did things to be successful. I put all my focus on solving problems because I knew this was strength of mine. I have always viewed problems as opportunities for growth. I cleared the big pile of crap off my desk and started to break down each and every part of the pharmacy to see where I could improve. The first piece I looked at was the business plan. I wanted to know what I said on the business plan and what I could do differently. Then I moved to marketing, sales, and what my customers wanted. Last, I moved to the employees, although this part was not in the business plan. Were they excited to sell and support the efforts of the business? Having happy employees gives the customer's confidence that they made the right decision to change.

Right when I started digging into the business, a patient came in and had some questions. Her name was Debbie and she was a cancer patient that had tons of questions about her treatments. While in pharmacy school we were taught a specific way to interview a patient and this tool we used is call the "SOAP Note". The SOAP Note was originally invented by Dr. Weed to get a brief statement about the patient's complaint, gather objective data to measure the patient's chief complaint, assess the findings and come up with a treatment plan for the patient. After my time with Debbie, I got back to my office and the light bulb came ON! Why not use the same method to systematically solve issues in a business. This is where I started to put together the S.O.A.P. Framework for business and began applying it to problems and systems in the business.

I told you about how the SOAP note works, now let me give you an explanation of the S.O.A.P. Framework for Business. Next, I will start applying it to some of the aspects of business and problems that we all face.

The S.O.A.P. Framework is a tool that I developed to help me identify and evaluate issues, problems and potential opportunities in the pharmacy. It has now grown into a tool that I use to teach entrepreneurs and business owners to identify, diagnose and cure business related pains and problems. The idea behind the S.O.A.P. Framework is to spot a potential issue and or problem and have a deep systematic way of solving it with efficiency and focus to get it right the first time. By having this tool, it allows the business owner to spend more time working on their business and increasing revenues while freeing up more time to spend on items of greater importance, like family.

When I talk about problems and issues that does not always mean there is a fire and it needs to be put out ASAP. A problem or issue could be that you want more sales, better training for your staff, or that you might need a complete makeover of the sales protocols. Maybe it's time to update the look of the business and change the logo for a fresh new look or maybe it really is a fire and you are losing a group of customers that think they don't want or need your products and services.

Let's get into the meaning of the S.O.A.P. Framework and really breakdown the different components so you can learn and start to use it in your businesses today. There are four parts to the S.O.A.P. Framework: Define the problem, identify causes of the problem, evaluate the findings and develop a solution to the problem.

Subjective = Define the pain

Subjective is gathering and reviewing data about a specific problem or issue that is causing pain to the business. It does not matter if it is a current problem or future problem. The two steps are the factors and elements.

The factors are a series of questions that need to be answered. They are: When did the problem start? Is the problem constant or has it gotten worse? What is the severity of the problem? Are there any modifying factors? What aggravates or reduces the issue and what other variables are contributing to the problem. What has been tried to fix the problem?

The elements are contributing factors to the problem. Every problem has one or all of the following elements that contribute it the issues. The elements are physical, human, and/or organizational. The physical is a piece of equipment that broke down and is causing stress to the problem or issue. Was the problem caused by a human element? Did someone do something wrong or neglect doing something that needed to be done? The last element is organizational. This means did the organization establish a policy; procedure, system, or process that helped people to make decisions or do their work was faulty?

Let's say, for example, your company's computer breaks down and you are unable to process orders. Not being able to process orders means that you are losing money left and right. What elements caused this issue? The physical is that a server broke down and the cash registers are not working.

This means no orders can be processed. The next step is to look at the human element. Someone did not clean the fans on the server which caused the computer to overheat and shut down. The third element is organizational. The IT department had protocols to do maintenance on the computers, but the protocol did not establish who was in charge of the maintenance for the computers on the third floor. This is a case of where one person thought someone else did the work, but in reality, no one did the work because the protocol was not clearly written. In this example, all three elements played a key role in the problem.

Objective = Identify the pain

This is the data collection phase to determine why this problem happened and document objective, repeatable and traceable facts about the problem.

Most company's stop after this phase, identifying one or two problems, but that normally is not sufficient. You want to make sure that you get to the root cause of the problem so you can make a plan to prevent it in the future.

The questions and data that need to be

asked and gathered in this phase are:

- What hard data is there to show a problem? An example: Profits are dropping, but sales are consistent with past months.

- How is the problem affecting your staff, customers, productions, or profits?

An example: Production cost has gone up because of the rise in gas prices and your prices have not been reevaluated in two years.

Here is a list of techniques to help get to the root cause. The first is "The 5 Whys by Sakichi Toyoda, The Drill Down Technique", and "The 5 Whats by Dr. Bernard Gramlich".

The 5 Whys is a technique of asking *why did it happen* in order to explore the cause and effect relationship to an underlying problem. One of Toyotas executives developed this technique to solve some of their manufacturing issues. The way it works is to ask the question of "Why" until you reach the root cause of your problem. One question that I get all the time is when do I stop with the why questions? Once the root cause has been revealed, then you stop. If that happens on the third why or the tenth why it does not matter, but normally the fifth one will reveal the root cause.

The Drill Down technique is used to break large amounts of data into smaller and smaller pieces to be easily understood. The process is to write down the larger problem on the left hand side of the paper and on the right side write down the points that detail the problem. With the drill down technique, keep asking questions until you fully understand the factors contributing to the problem. By drilling into a question it helps you build a much deeper understanding of the problem and it helps link information about the issues that you may not have initially associated with the problem.

I am a "What" kind of person and I caught myself asking the same five questions when a problem popped up in my business. The five "What" questions are my own creation that I have used through the years to help me get to the root cause of a problem or issue that I was having in my business.

- What is causing the problem? What or who is suffering from the problem or proposed change?

- What is being affected and how? What is the problem or change affecting in the business, employees or clients?

- What is the impact of this problem on the business? Compute the input and output of the problem or change.

- What do you need input from to solve the problem or create a change? Do I need to hire an outside consultant, interview employees, or survey clients to get to a positive change?

- What are the limitations that will impact the solution for success of this problem? Is there a lack of cash flow, regulation changes, not enough manpower, or lack of expertise and knowledge preventing success?

Assessment = Evaluate and find a solution for the pain

In the assessment phase, you now evaluate all the information gathered in the first two phases and start to develop *multiple* solutions for the problem. A very important part of the assessment phase is getting input from the whole team. Getting input from everyone gives a wider variety of possible solutions.

You will want to find the following:

The solution should evaluate the impact on the business and provide an answer for H.E.R.D.

H.E.R.D. Stands for Hours, Emotions, Relationships, and Dollars.

- The solution should measure the impact on the amount of *hours* gained or lost due to the problem or issue.

- How is the issue or problem affecting the *emotional* state of the staff, management, and you? Is it causing stress, sleepless nights, or anxiety between members of the staff?

- How is it impacting the *relationships* between the company and your vendors, from employee to employee, or the impact on you and your family?

- How is this problem affecting the *(dollars)* top and bottom line on the profit and loss statement?

There are several key points to remember in the assessment phase. The solution should make the business better, review current systems for flaws, solve one problem at a time, clearly state a single solution, and develop a plan for accountability and prevention.

Plan = Solve the pain

In the plan phase, take one of the answers and put it into action. The steps that need to be taken in this phase:

1. How will the solution be implemented?
2. How to prevent this problem from happening again?
3. What are the risk factors involved with this answer?
4. Who is responsible for it?
5. Hold someone accountable.
6. Develop a follow up with a system to ensure that the plan is working and working right
7. If not, then be ready with a plan "B"

You will always have issues and problems in your business. Do not run away from them. Welcome the issues and problems because they will help you and your team seek new and improved ways to run the business.

By using the S.O.A.P. Framework to solve

your business related problems, there are some key elements to keep in mind are to support your process. All processes need to have an owner, formal process for data measurement, reporting the data and resources allocated to ensure timely evaluations and improvements. Some useful tactics are:

- The need for improvement and willingness to engage in tough conversations with your employees, vendors, and management.

- Staying focused on the objective.

- Looking for signs of resistance.

- Helping the staff move from resistance to action.

- Reward success.

- Getting feedback from the staff, customers, and team for further improvements.

By asking these questions before you execute your plan, you will be able to identify the changes needed for various systems. It is also important to plan ahead to predict the effects of this solution and, hopefully, help you spot potential failures before they happen.

To keep the business systems and operations from being outdated and inefficient, take extra time to evaluate new technologies, trends in the industry, and establish new goals to keep pace with the business world. If you do not keep your finger on the pulse, your business will get left behind.

Humans and businesses are both living breathing things. Just like you go to the doctor for yearly checkups, your business needs to get checkups to maintain the health of the business. Your clients, employees, and family are depending on you to use every tool at your disposal to be successful and keep a healthy business.

In the next chapter, I will apply the S.O.A.P. Framework to the Business Plan and explain the good, the bad and the ugly with why you should have one as opposed to those who say you don't need one.

Chapter 4

The Active Business Plan

Bloomberg reports that eight out of 10 startup businesses will fail within the first 18 months. Why do they fail? What can we learn from their failures? What can we apply to our businesses *today* to ensure a fighting chance at success?

Many experts say that entrepreneurs fail because they run out of money. I say, "Really? That's the best you have?" I hate to burst everyone's bubble, but businesses don't fail. The entrepreneur fails, and the business is just a casualty. They failed because they did not make a plan for success. Benjamin Franklin said, "If you fail to plan, you are planning to fail." This is really how I feel about business plans. Developing a business plan gives benefits beyond just trying to get financing. It takes the emotion out of the business and focuses on the work. The actual written paper is not as important as the process of developing the plan. Later, you can follow up by comparing the plan to the actual business and using it to measure the results and make corrections where they are needed.

The failure to keep the doors open starts long before running out of money. If the entrepreneur had sat down and written out a plan of attack, some of the questions, problems and surprises would have been eliminated. Maybe the company failed because the owner did not listen to the customers very well. Maybe the business just shoved its product down customers' throats.

Walking in your customer's shoes is a great way to understand what they want and how you should present to them. Maybe you did not take the time to review your competition and find a way to differentiate your business from theirs. You do not have to reinvent the wheel. You just need to find a way to make it unique.

The simplest definition of a business plan is a guide or roadmap for your business that outlines goals and details a plan for you to achieve those goals. This is the one that you take to the bank to get financing for your business. I don't feel that you need to have a 50-page business plan to be successful. I have seen some that are quite impressive with the fancy binder and super graphics, but a simple business plan can lead you to success.

A good business plan will help guide you through the business operations from pre-opening to selling the business. It is a path that helps keeps clarity and focus on the goals ahead without living on emotions for the business. Being emotional is great if you are having a baby, but when opening a business, the focus need to be razor sharp. Some of the questions that I like to answer in my business plan are:

1. What is the concept?
2. Research questions
    a. Location
    b. Competition
    c. Office furniture
    d. All the little things that are needed to run an office.
3. How am I going to market it?
4. What am I going to sell?
5. What is the cost to make and sell my product or service?
6. What is going to happen on day one?

7. What is my pricing? What gross margin do I want to make?

8. How am I going to get traffic?

9. How long will it take to close one sale?

10. What are my financial projections (quarterly for the first year, then yearly for three years)?

I love to have a personal plan to go along with my business plan. The business plan outlines the goals for the business and your personal plan should outline your personal goals for the business and family. What do you want from your life? Do you want weekends off? Do you want to spend more time with the family? Trust me when I say that all the money in the world will not mean a thing, if you can't enjoy it. Working yourself into the ground and missing out on key components of life are things that you can never get back once they are gone. Time is the focus in the life plan. How do you want to spend your time?

When Marisol and I had our first son Liam, I was so focused on growing my pharmacy to my personal goal of $10 million a year that I missed out on many moments with Liam that I had to learn about from video or Facebook. I look back at that time in my life, and it pains me to know that I missed those awesome moments. If you take nothing else out of this chapter, please take the time to understand that time is the one thing you can never get back and to please use it wisely.

Now, let's get to the substance of the business plan. This should be a plan that establishes a path with a set of goals that are attainable. The business plan should also contain information about you and your team (if you have one) and background on your competition. The other crucial element in your business plan is your financials, based on cash flow and not sales. Completing the financials and understanding cash flow is difficult. Most entrepreneurs – both young and wiser (a term I use to make myself feel less old) – confuse cash flow with sales. They think that by having high sales, you are successful. I will spend more time on sales in Chapter 8. But, for now, the reason you must have quality cash flow is because no one starts a business with unlimited cash in the bank. You must have enough cash to last long enough to have a viable business. A viable business is one that is able to pay the bills, give you a salary and have some left over for growth.

The question that many entrepreneurs ask is, "Why have a business plan?" There are many theories on this topic. William Gartner, a professor from Clemson University, believes that it is essential to have a business plan. He noted that on the SBA website, "The importance of a comprehensive, thoughtful business plan can not be over-emphasized". On the flip side, there have been many others that have said that business plans are not essential and you can be successful without one. But, in a recent study done by the Panel Study of Entrepreneurial Dynamics, a national study of more than 800 people that started a business, they found that writing a plan greatly increased the chances of success.

I am a success story and victim of doing and not doing a business plan. I am going to share each story with you and apply the S.O.A.P. Framework to it to show the function of the S.O.A.P Framework in the business plan process.

My first story is the story of not having a business plan and how it led to disaster. Remember in Chapter 2 when I told you about the ice cream store I opened in North Hollywood, California? This business was started with my ex-wife and her brother. I will call them Sue and Bob for the purposes of this story. We were family, so I figured that we had a built in trust. We had discussions prior to the opening so we knew what we were going to do and how we were going to get there. Oh, how wrong I was! The way we talked about setting up the business was that we were going to divide the business up into three parts. I was going to take care of the sales and internal business side of the store. Bob was going to run the daily operations in the store and Sue was going to handle the banking. For the first couple of months, things seemed to be working just fine and the business was starting to grow. It seemed like the problems that popped up were somewhat small and could be solved quickly. Again, oh, how wrong I was! I was under the impression that Bob was handling the new vendors and taking care of the customers the way I would if I was in the store and that Sue was making the daily deposits and keeping track of the daily sales, the way we discussed in the beginning. Well, the business was now growing, and the money did not seem to be going into the bank the way it should have been according to the original plan.

    I was in school at we had prior to opening. I blame myself for this failure because I knew that we should have written the rules, goals, and pathway down on paper, but I figured they knew what they were doing. Hell, I figured I knew what I was doing. Four months

Chapter 4 | The Active Business Plan

in, I wrote a basic plan to follow to grow the business, but there had been so much damage to the relationships with the vendors and between us that they were resistant to any plan I put up for us to follow. We did fight through the tension and grew the business to a great revenue-producing store even with strained relationships. I would loved to have seen how the business would have grown if we would have worked together instead of against each other.

The quality of the problem was a major one because it affected sales, employees, customers, and our relationship to work together. The severity of the problem was severe! I say this because as we continued on, more problems started to develop from the original issue of not putting together a business plan. Almost everything we did to grow the business back fired and that aggravated every other part of the business and really held us back.

Now, within the Subjective phase of S.O.A.P Framework, I like to figure out if the problem was physical, human, or organizational or any part or all three. In this case, the problem was human and organizational. The human element of it was that we did not sit down and write out a proper path for where the business was going and what our roles were in the business. We should have established policies and procedures for many of the items you need when running a business. We did not plan out how we were going to handle marketing, sales or employees. We really did this off the cuff. Even though I was the only one with business experience, I was still pretty green at that time and did not have a strong enough hand. We were using the Band-Aid method to fix the issues we had. The Band-Aid method is to just stop the immediate problem without taking the time to dig down and identify the real issue. We were in full Band-Aid mode because we did not stop to sit down and figure out what was going on.

    The best example of a company not using the Band-Aid method of solving a problem is Howard Schultz and Starbucks. Howard had left Starbucks for some time, and the company started to fall apart. The board asked him to come back, and when he did, the transformation was awesome. He set up a conference call with every associate that worked for Starbucks and closed every store for a few hours to retrain staff, share the new direction and clear up any confusion. Since then, Starbucks has grown into a monster of a company because they have a clear-cut leader and clear-cut goals.

The next part is the Objective phase of the S.O.A.P Framework. Here is where you start to gather objective data about your issue or problem. In our case, we failed to do a business plan and our communication and focus was not where it needed to be to run a successful company. We knew there were problems because the sales were growing, but the cash flow was horrible, the employees and vendors were not happy, and we were dropping the ball on projects that needed to get done. Again we all had serious communication failures and lack of focus. This led to us all working on the same parts. This spells disaster! We did customer surveys, and they were not pretty. They were saying the service was slow and the employees looked confused about what they should be doing.

Another problem we had was that no one was looking at these surveys to fix the problems faster. Our vendors were also not happy. They were getting paid late, and our purchases were dropping with our largest vendor even though sales were growing. There was no reporting or even follow-up with the vendors.

At this point, we could have started using the 'five whys system' to help explore the cause and effect relationship between the vendors complaining and why our vendor list was growing. We could have used the *drill-down technique* with the five whys and made a list of all the little problems that were popping up and traced them back to failure to plan. The business plan would have given us the focus we needed to stay on track with the task that each of us should have been handling.

The next part is the Assessment Phase. This is where after identifying the problem to the root cause; you start to develop multiple solutions for the issue or problem. The root cause of our problem at the ice cream store was a lack of focus, communication or a proper path to follow. Here, we should have sat down and come up with multiple solutions for our problems. Some of the solutions could have been to develop a business plan that outlined the management team and their roles, the outside sales process, inside sales process, how inventory was going to be handled and the financials. By taking a step back like Howard Schultz did with Starbucks, we would have put ourselves in a much better position for success. We could have taken some time to review what was working and what was not working to make a stronger plan. This is the exact reason why the business plan is a living, breathing document. After you write it down, don't just put in the safe and never look at it again. That would defeat the purpose of having this awesome plan you just wrote.

In the Assessment phase, it is crucial to identify:

1. Does the issue address more than one problem?
    a. In the case of the ice cream store, yes it did.
        ii. Management team disorganization
        iii. No meeting schedule
        iv. No sales process inside or outside
        v. No policies and procedures
        vi. No inventory protocols
        vii. No banking protocols
2. Does the problem assign a cause?
    a. Yes it did. It caused the system to fail.
        ii. Losing customers

S.O.A.P. Framework

        iii. Unhappy vendors

        iv. Unhappy management

3. Can the problem assign blame?

    a. Yes, because as a group we did not do a business plan that would have created a path for us to follow.

4. Did the problem offer a solution?

    a. This is a hard one because I was only a part-time piece of the puzzle and if I had not gotten the call when I did from the vendor, it may not have prompted me to act as fast as I did to try to save the business.

The next step in the Assessment phase is to get the team to agree that there is a problem, that we can agree on a solution to the problem and, most importantly, that we can hold a team member accountable for the solution and for them to be able to recognize if it is or is not working in the best interest of the business.

Now, we have reached the Plan Phase. In the plan phase, we take one of the many solutions and put it into action. We decided to get a business plan done and that would give

CHAPTER 4 | THE ACTIVE BUSINESS PLAN

us the focus and clarity we needed to get the business to the next level. The next level for us was to be able to run the business smoothly and have a clear direction for the business.

Along with the business plan, we wrote we answered the following questions.

1. How do we prevent this problem from happening again?

    a. Did we accomplish this by agreeing to add an addendum to the plan every time we wanted to add a new piece of business?

        i. For example, I was able to be the coffee and ice cream supplier for some major motion pictures.

2. How will the solution be implemented?

    a. We agreed to sit down every week and discuss the news of the business. We went over each of the tasks that we were in charge of for the week and any questions or concerns we had with customers or vendors.

    b. We assigned all new activities to a responsible team member.

    c. We assessed the risk factors with

developing a new plan and all the new policies and procedures along with how they were going to affect the customers and vendors.

3. The last thing is to support the plan with a formal process that can be measured and reported.

    a. Now, adjustments can be made with ease.

    b. Now, the tough conversations aren't as tough because everyone is one the same page.

    c. Keeps you focused on the objective.

    d. Helped us find signs of resistance.

        i. With this we could see if the customers and vendors were happy.

        ii. If we got some pushback from the staff, was it because they did not fit into the culture or were we not being realistic with our goals and expectations?

        iii. If it was the staff, we could retrain them to move from resistance to action and of that did not work then we knew we had to cut them loose.

d. We set up a reward process for the employees.

    v. This kept them motivated to perform at the highest level.

f. Set up a feedback loop so that customers, vendors, staff, and our team could evaluate our ideas for improvement or dislike for a new procedure.

Now that we had the Plan in place to write a new business plan, we were able to stay together for another year before I sold my part to them and got out of the ice cream business. During that year, we were able to execute the business plan to near perfection. Maybe I am a little bias, but we did grow the business from 5k per month in sales to over 33k per month in sales with a gross margin of 34%. We had built a great customer base and also went out and got other streams of revenue by supplying coffee and ice cream to the movie studios. We even got Ice Cube to shoot a scene from his movie *Players Club*. These extra sources of income were a great way to think outside the box and grow the brand and culture of the business. And, yes, I did add in the new protocols for each of the outside the box revenue streams.

The benefits of taking a step back and writing a business plan even after we had been open for about four months is that we were able to take a business that was destined to fail sooner and make it into a profitable business. The other benefits are that it created a better working relationship between us, the team, and every other aspect of the business from customers to vendors.

One of the best parts, in my opinion, is that all of the new ideas were analyzed and broken down to see if that business would fit into the culture we were building with our brand. I strongly suggest that if you do not have a business plan, write one, even if you are already in business and making money. The benefits of having a plan on how you want to run the business and having to writing down is PRICELESS!

The next chapter will discuss marketing and how the S.O.A.P. Framework can be applied to marketing. I have a couple of examples with my business and some from clients that I can share.

Chapter 5

Marketing Strategies with S.O.A.P.

In the last chapter, I told a story about my ice cream store named *IScream* and how not having a business plan really hurt us in the beginning of the business. So, trust me, when I say at the start of my next business, I had a business plan and personal plan written and ready to go on day one of Cedar Pharmacy. Business plan in hand, I was ready to go out and market the business to the community. All I had to do was wait for my permit from the State Board of Pharmacy to give me the go ahead and open. Finally, at the end of January of 2003, I got the permit and I was ready to open. When day one rolled around and I opened the doors, I was just waiting for a flood of patients to start pouring in.

Guess what? They didn't! My plan said that I was in a medical building and the patients would leave their doctor's offices, see my tiny little sign and come in to get their medications and other healthcare supplies from Cedar Pharmacy. My marketing plan was built on the fact that the patients already had trust in the pharmacy and some 'hope marketing'. Not sure if you have heard of *'hope marketing'* before, but it is where you sit and *hope* customers walk in your business to purchase goods and services. The true definition is that it is the kind of marketing that gets you nothing. On my first day, I sat there and sat and sat and sat, and then my first patient walked in! *Oh my God! What do I do?* I was so excited that I dropped my glass of water on the counter and tripped over my chair trying to get to the front counter to greet her. The best part is that she was a dentist in the building and she helped me to relax. We talked about the ins and outs of the building. This did not help me with my marketing plan, but it did help me focus my efforts on how to get patients in the door after we talked about the building and who was who. She told me some of the ways that she was able to attract new patients when she opened her doors twenty years before. Over the next few days, I wrote out how I was going to build trust, build traffic and be the best pharmacy on the block. I call that my *marketing funnel*. I had to plan out how to be unique because I had four major chain pharmacy stores within a five-mile radius of my 900-square foot pharmacy. How could I tweak the pharmacy just enough not to scare people away and get them to love what I had to offer?

Having a solid marketing plan helps build the focus needed to grow a business from nothing to being viable. Let me quickly define *'viable'* for you. *Viable* is a business that makes enough money to pay its bills, pay you a salary, and leaves enough left over for growth. Let's get back to the marketing plan. The plan links the service or product to a group of people that are willing to buy from you. This plan also gives a path to get traffic and take the emotion out of it so you don't do what I did and trip and fall in front of your first customer.

In this chapter, I am going to define marketing and share my ideas on how marketing should be done. I will discuss the importance of having a properly working marketing funnel (which I will redefine later) and where most businesses fail in the marketing funnel process. Of course, I will apply the S.O.A.P. Framework to help explain some of my businesses as well as some clients businesses.

By definition, marketing is the field of management devoted to selling. It connects the link between production and profit, while taking the product or service through the most appropriate channels to find the people most likely to buy it. To fulfill this goal is the tough part. You have to be skilled at understanding the market. This means closely studying the lifestyle and behavior of the potential customers so that the product or service can be developed to be attractive in every way. You have to focus on the purpose, function, quality, appearance, speed at which the product will be delivered, where it will be sold, the price, down to the level of customer service and support offered.

Okay, now we have the technical definition of marketing that covers the checklist of things to do to be successful. Marketing is not guaranteed to work, but if you use the checklist, it should increase your chances of reaching the goals you have set for the business and becoming successful more times than not. In my case, I could not just market myself as a pharmacy. I mean, the drugs are the same; the copays are the same, and all pharmacies promise great customer service. I know you're laughing right now thinking the top three chain pharmacies providing great customer service. It was hard for me to write that part, but they try... I think. So, what could I do that would separate me from the pack without reinventing the wheel? I had to make something in my marketing plan that was unique and worth talking about. I wanted something worth noticing and something new that could help make Cedar Pharmacy the "it place" to get your medications from instead of the competitors.

Now, I had my work cut out for me. I studied the patients, the doctors in the building and what my competitors were doing, and I started putting my funnel together to get people coming in. A marketing funnel is not a new kitchen tool; it is an avenue to attract and engage clients to purchase your product or service. It also lets you know where your company needs to jump in and influence the customer at each stage of the funnel. See figure 1 for the stages. My problem with the funnel is that it does not help maintain the customer. Once the person buys, he or she is dropped off the sales point and is gone.

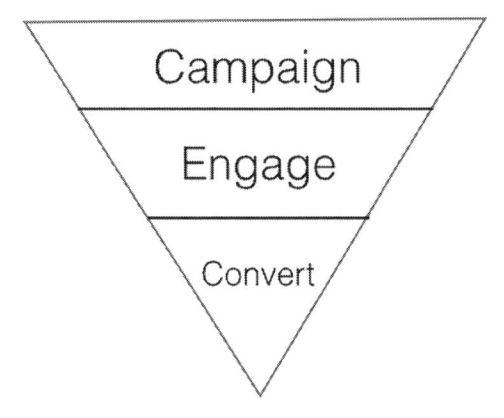

Figure 1. Marketing Funnel.

Being in the healthcare profession, I like to think in terms of health. I use the Customer Life Cycle. The Customer Life Cycle is where the customer is the center of your world and everything you do depends on one or all of three things:

1. What does the customer want?

2. What does the customer need?

3. What do they need and want that they don't know about yet?

Sometimes you will need to step outside and give the customers something they don't know they need. The perfect example of this is the iPad. Steve Jobs did not make this product because people were asking for it. He made the iPad because he saw a way to revolutionize the travel-computing world. But, that's a whole

CHAPTER 5 | MARKETING STRATEGIES WITH S.O.A.P.

new world that we can talk about later in life. The most common area where businesses fail in the marketing funnel is the content to entice the customer to purchase. They are not able to get the customer from the campaign to convert. They get stuck or fall out of the engagement part of the funnel. If your content is not compelling enough to keep the customers' interest, they will leave you and go elsewhere to satisfy their curiosity.

The Customer life cycle will build loyalty, increase repeat sales and, most importantly, get people talking about your product or service.

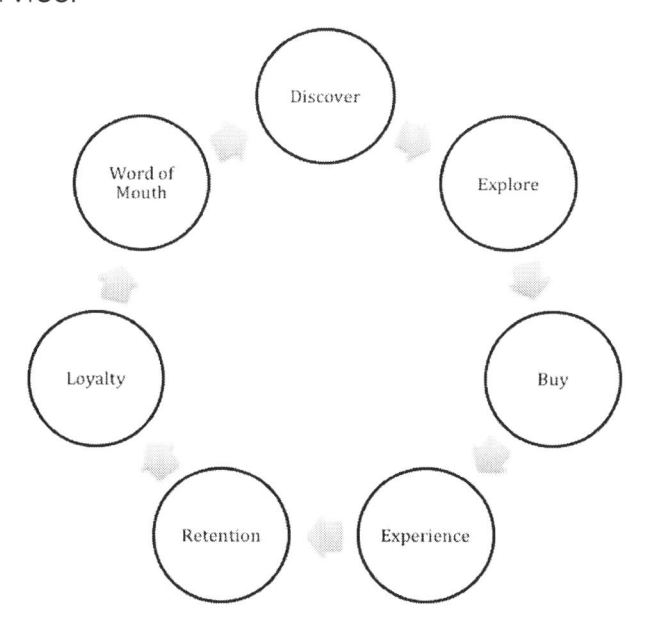

Figure 2 The Customer Life Cycle

You start with a marketing funnel to get people to see the business and pique their interest in your products or services. Then, you gently guide them into your Customer life Cycle to get a lifetime of sales from them.

I wanted to do more than 5-10 prescriptions a day. I had the goal to be filling 100 prescriptions a day by the end of the first quarter and 300 a day by the end of one year. I knew I was not getting there by *hope marketing*, so I sat down and applied the S.O.A.P. Framework to my problem of little traffic due to a poor marketing plan.

Subjective

The problem that I wanted to solve was to grow the business and establish a solid marketing plan to reach the prescription and sales goals, still keeping cash flow and gross margin in mind.

- The onset of the problem started day one, but I did not realize it until about three weeks later.
- The sales numbers did not really go up or down by very much, regardless of the things I was trying in the beginning. I was acting just like the chain pharmacies. I promised great service, and so did they. I promised short wait times, and so did

they. I was not doing anything to be unique.

- I could tell that the problem of not having sales and cash flow was going to bankrupt me in a matter of months.

- In this example, the additional factors were human and organizational:

    o Human: My original marketing plan was vague and not unique.

    o Organizational: I had enough experience at that point to write a better plan but just dropped the ball because I felt the location was going to carry me further.

- I tried to meet and greet the patients and doctors. This helped build trust, but not loyalty and sales.

Objective

I was getting plenty of engagement, but not converting them to sales. The plan in place was not getting people in the door and selling them. The data that cemented this was the fact that my sales and cash flow were not growing.

- I knew there was a problem because of the lack of sales.

- I had people walking into the pharmacy

and asking questions, but not enough were talking about their experience with me and purchasing products.

- The problem was affecting the bottom line and the fear that the pharmacy would go under.

- Using the 5 Whys Approach

    o Why are we not getting customers?
        - Because they are set in their ways and there is no need to change.
    o Why won't they change?
        - Because there has not been a link of trust built.
    o Why has there not been a link of trust built?
        - Because the marketing plan was too vague and it needs to be updated to meet the needs of the clients we seek.
    o Why was the marketing plan not thorough enough?
        - Because of poor research in the beginning before opening the business.

After the fourth one in this case, I was able to see where the problem was. Now, in the

Assessment phase, I can start to provide some solutions to correct the issue.

Assessment

Now, that I had identified the problem, it was time to develop a few solutions to get the pharmacy to the viable state.

Proposed solutions

1. Start an outbound marketing campaign that has mailers and flyers.

2. Start an inbound marketing campaign and try to attract people via the web.

3. Continue visiting the doctors' offices and leaving flyers.

4. Make better signage.

5. Go to the health fairs and be more visible.

6. Create a unique buzz that would prompt people to talk about the pharmacy.

    a. Give green vials instead of the normal amber vials every other pharmacy uses.

7. Start compounding medications that are custom to the patient

    a. Bio-Identical Hormone

Replacement Therapy (BHRT) for women and men.

   b. Pain medications.

8. Start a delivery service for patients that cannot travel to pharmacy to get their medications.

Now that I had eight solutions to start with, it was time to weed out the ones that wouldn't work and prioritize the ones that might.

Plan

From the Assessment phase, I had eight options that I thought of at the time and I eliminated number one because it was too expensive. There is also little return on outbound marketing in today's markets. With the remaining options, I decided to prioritize them into ones that I felt I could get a return on my investment. My list was 6, 3, 2, 4, 8, 5, 7. I wanted to start simple so I switched the vials from amber to green. Another reason was that it went along with my cedar tree logo and whole green pharmacy theme. By doing a simple little tweak like changing the vials, I was not expecting a huge response but a little bump. It ended up being a huge success because patients were now walking in and asking, *"Hey, are you the place that has green bottles?"* Shocking, but it worked, and people came to get their meds in green bottles because they were different and the best part is they were talking about the pharmacy.

Under the Plan Phase, there are a few things that you should address besides just selecting a solution.

1. How can I prevent my marketing woes from happening again?

    a. By taking the business plan with the marketing section and using it as an active document. If I stay on top of the numbers for the business I will be able to see when new marketing efforts are needed or just tweaks to the old ones.

2. How will the prioritized solutions be implemented?

    a. After I started with the green vials the next one would go into effect two weeks later. I set time frames to some items and net cash flow increases for others.

3. Since I was the face of the company I was responsible for the plan and following it through to the end.

    a. The only sucky part about not

having a team is that your ideas are it. But, that is where if I had not been a stubborn fool I could have consulted with other small business owners or a consultant.

4. The biggest risk factor was that it would not work. I started small and worked my way up to the more expensive ways of marketing because I wanted to make sure that cash was not going to be the reason for the business failing.

5. The follow-up system that I had in place was tracking the data on an excel spreadsheet and following the numbers on my QuickBooks. Using the business plan as a dynamic document was another huge key to the solution.

The other pieces of the Plan phase are to watch for resistance from the customers that would lead to lack of growth. By following these steps, it really helped me to stay focused on the goal of growth and building the patient base. The stronger the patient base, the more prescriptions, which in turn means increases in sales and one step closer to viability. The best part of the Plan phase is that you get to reward yourself. Taking 5-10 minutes a day to pat yourself on the back. It goes a long way to maintaining mental health when running a start-up.

As you can see, the benefits of using the S.O.A.P Framework to solve your problem is that it gave me a path and working document to drive the marketing efforts in the right direction. In the beginning, my plan was vague and now the plan was clear, concise and I ready to kick butt. By following this marketing path, I was able to exceed my sales, prescription counts, and gross margin goals that I set for myself. I was able to break $668,000 in my first year and $1 million in sales after fourteen months. With the right marketing plan and some hard work, I was able to grow the sales and reach my first mini goal of $1 million.

Most people think that being a small start-up pharmacy competing against the larger big box retailers puts them behind the eight ball from the get go, but that is only the truth if you let it. Believing in yourself to compete will take you and your business a long way. I never let fear and being ordinary rule my world. If I did, failure would have been at the top of the list. You will make mistakes and you will have failures, but you don't quit. You should keep fighting for the next thing that will help your success. Never let fear or the negative influence from people tell you what will work and what won't work.

Take, for example, the Volkswagen Beetle that was first built in 1938. When it first came out, it was not the counterculture car that people remember. It took expensive TV ads and tons of print campaigns to save the car and turn it into the pop culture icon that we remember. This car was the poster child of the old outbound marketing ways to get people to notice your product or service. The 1997-present VW Beetle, on the other hand, used a bit of old school marketing as it relied on inbound marketing for its success. The success was built on the great reviews, awesome word of mouth and the way it looked: a round car in a square world. Just think about every time you saw a new VW Beetle drive by you on the freeway. I know you made some kind of comment and probably told someone somewhere about this new car you just saw. Look at all that free marketing.

That is what you want for your business: free marketing and marketing your product in the sense that makes it different. I know that changing the vials from amber to green was not the biggest reason for my success in the pharmacy, but it was start. You need to get out there and just start. Don't let fear of change or being unprepared stop you from trying new and different marketing ideas.

In the next chapter, I am going to discuss the business strategy part of business and how these will change and grow as the business grows. I will outline the successes and failures of some businesses that had either weak strategies or no strategies in place.

CHAPTER 6

Business Strategies Using S.O.A.P.

When I was growing up, I would watch old war movies. The generals from each side were always talking about strategy. Strategy, in this sense, is a military concept of positioning your soldiers in better places than your enemy's so they can be defeated with ease. In business theory, strategy is an overused and misunderstood word. Today when a company has a new product that they want to get into the public's hands, they start the strategy session. In that strategy session, the company's brass wants to identify where they are and how to get where they want to be. This involves identifying the choices that must be made to overcome the obstacles that are in the way of their success. In these sessions, the company's choosing *what not to do is just as important as what to do*. This was a point that was brought to the light by Michael

Chapter 6 | Business Strategies Using S.O.A.P.

Porter in "What is Strategy."

In my businesses and for some of my clients I have worked with, it is just as possible to follow a bad strategy, as it is to follow a good strategy. To establish a good strategy, a company should do a complete analysis of its current production and its goals. They should use the SWOT framework (strengths, weaknesses, opportunities, threats), the most popular system for this type of audit. For it to be completely effective, everyone from middle management up to the CEO should conduct it. When a company is evaluating a new way to go, it will require that they analyze their competition and any threats to the company. This may involve some tough conversations with processes, policies, and personnel. A company that capitalizes on its strengths and has clear-cut goals when developing a strong strategy can be flexible in the new course they are taking and will have a better chance at success.

On the flipside, a bad strategy goes hand in hand with the simple Band-Aid type of goal or vision for a new product or service. How many times have you seen a CEO stand up on the stage and give a great motivational speech about all the new changes coming in the next year only to be based on unrealistic goals? I have to say I have experienced this personally from two major corporations that I worked with earlier in my career. In fact, one company's stock went from $51 a share to 25 cents a share due to very poor strategies and extremely poor management. They ignored problems and were blinded to the choices they were making. Rather than making some tough decisions to correct the issues, they decided to continue with the plan and not really deal with any of the conflicting demands from the newfound strategy. When these types of strategies are employed, the managers tend to stick to the same old way and they don't take any initiative to lead and come up with new ideas.

Being able to put a strong strategy together for the people of your company to follow is very important because it gives them a sense of power and focus to get the job done and done right. If the employee does not trust your judgment or the path that the new idea is going, the follow through will be spotty at best. This begs the question: *Are you a leader or a manager? What is the difference between a manager and leader?*

Managers have subordinates

Authoritarian: Managers are in a position of authority given to them by the company, and their subordinate's work for them and largely do as they are told. Managers tell the subordinate what to do, and the subordinate does this not because they are a blind robot. They follow because they have been promised a reward (at minimum their salary) for doing so.

Work focus: Managers are paid to get things done (they are subordinates too), often within tight constraints of time and money.

Seek comfort: An interesting research finding about managers is that they tend to come from stable home backgrounds and led relatively normal and comfortable lives. This leads them to be relatively risk-averse and they will seek to avoid conflict where possible. In terms of people, they generally like to run a 'happy ship'.

Leaders have followers

Leaders do not have subordinates - at least not when they are leading.

Charismatic: Leaders with a stronger

charisma find it easier to attract people to their cause. As a part of their persuasion, they typically promise transformational benefits, such that their followers will not just receive extrinsic rewards, but will somehow become better people.

People focus: Although leaders are good with people, this does not mean they are friendly with them. In order to keep the mystique of leadership, they often retain a degree of separation and aloofness.

As an entrepreneur, I am sure that somewhere along the way you have heard the term *'business strategy'* used. But, what exactly is a *business strategy*? Business strategy means to establish a set of goals to reach a desired objective. The problem is that most business leaders and theorists have many different definitions for what business strategy means and most still argue about the topic and have not come up with a definitive answer. I think the reason is because we all think about strategy in different ways. Many entrepreneurs believe that you must analyze the company's present condition, anticipate any changes in the industry and how to move forward from this plan. On the other side, there are plenty of businessmen and women that feel the future is too difficult to predict and that your company should evolve as things change. I feel that if you can keep your finger on the pulse of your business by watching the numbers and reviewing the processes in which things are being handled, you as the decision maker can make a change before the problem starts.

Johnson and Scholes, authors of "Exploring Corporate Strategy," say that strategy determines the direction and scope of an organization over the long term, and they say that it should determine how resources should be configured to meet the needs of markets and stakeholders.

I mentioned Michael Porter earlier, and he is a strategy expert and professor at Harvard Business School who emphasizes the need for strategy to define and communicate an organization's unique position. He says that it should determine how organizational resources, skills, and competencies should be combined to create competitive advantage.

Success of your company will require you to have the ability and know how to evolve your strategy as the business landscape changes. Planning for success in your industry is important and to take full advantage of the opportunities that present themselves would require the company to prepare for the future on every level. This is where having the S.O.A.P. Framework in place with other business strategy tools will help keep your company on the cutting edge and moving toward viability and success.

Throughout the company there should be multiple levels of strategy development. One to look at the big picture, one for individual markets and one for day to day operations to help keep the company moving in the right direction. So, after that long-winded definition, the simple version is "determining how the company is going to succeed in the future."

I am going to apply the S.O.A.P. Framework to the demise of Kodak. Kodak employed a business strategy that took them from being the king of the hill to goats of the industry. Since this is a company that I have not worked with, I will be adding my own take on what I feel they should have done to save their company.

Subjective

The problem that I want to solve is, should Kodak have moved from the mainstay of film that was very profitable for them and/or setup a division to help move the company into the digital world?

- The onset of the problem started back in the 1970s.
    - Kodak engineers invented the digital camera.
- The problem slowly got worse because the senior management was ignoring this opportunity.
- The quality of the problem was that sales and recognition were decreasing year by year.
- It is easy now to say that the severity was MAJOR. They went bankrupt.
- The modifying factors were that the competition was swooping in on the technology while Kodak stood still and watched.
- The additional factors to consider would be
    - Human
        - The upper management of Kodak felt that the golden goose of film would keep the company alive and that digital was just a phase.
        - Very poor strategic thinking and not evaluating the future of their industry.

- o Organizational
    - The executives failed to see the digital photography would film redundant and challenge their near monopoly business.

Objective

The problem is that Kodak saw a drop in revenue because more and more people started to move over to digital instead of film.

- Kodak knew there was problem because a Japanese company FujiFilm saw the opportunity and diversified their company successfully.

- To everyone in the world – other than upper management at Kodak – the problem was clear and actionable.

- The problem was affecting the company's sales and the strategic team was providing solutions that were costly and ineffective.

- Kodak failed to realize that women were no longer the main users of the camera. Once digital came out men started to dominate the market.

Assessment

The basic problem was that Kodak did not want to let go of film and move into a digital world, although they invented the digital camera. It is a shame because Kodak was the company that took the camera out of the professional hands and put it into the hands of the responsible woman of the family to get that Kodak moment at the family event or vacation.

The solutions that Kodak came up with were:

1. People will never depart from using hard prints and will always value film-based photos for their high quality. Digital will just be a substitute for film-based photos.

2. The mindset will not change with cameras. The digital camera will be a toy compared to the original pure photographic equipment.

3. No one will be able to compete with Kodak's digital camera because they have the market share.

4. We will continue to advertise to women because they are the main customers of Kodak.

5. Create new mediums

    a. Photo CD

    b. Smaller cameras

    c. Digitally coded film

6. Create Kodak gallery. A weak attempt at generating revenue from digital images. The site was essentially a digital version of its analogue offerings. Digital's potential was never fully realized at Kodak.

7. Advertise to clients to use Kodak cameras, save the pictures on Kodak memory cards, put them on Kodak paper through Kodak printers, and edit them on in store Kodak digital kiosk.

8. Ignore the new technology because it will fade away.

    a. Their strategy here was to say it was too expensive, too slow, and too complicated.

9. Invest in a young start-up company that can help take them into the digital world. There were plenty of small powerful start-ups in the Silicon Valley that could have helped Kodak stay relevant.

Plan

Unfortunately, Kodak followed a template used by many companies before them that faced technological challenges and changes to their industries and they all failed because they did not look to the future and grasp the change to stay viable. At first, Kodak tried to ignore the new technology, hoping it would go away by itself. Then they tried to use various justifications that the technology was too expensive, too slow, or too complicated. After that, they try to prolong the life of the existing technology by attempting to create synergies between the new technology and the old (like Photo CD). By doing this, they delayed any serious commitment to changing the direction of the company. Bad strategy!

Some say that when Kodak was dabbling in digital versions of its analogue products, Kodak should have also invested in several start-ups based in Silicon Valley. The Silicon Valley Company would not have been weighted down by Kodak's legacy or its emotional attachment to the brand, and its product-based mentality. Most of the Silicon Valley Companies were led by entrepreneurs on a shoestring budget and they would have been led by people who get digital. They would have been comfortable with pitfalls and growing pains and would have tested tons of new digital models to find the right one that would have worked for the Kodak culture. They could have also made products that the new type of customer would have understood. Since they did not live in that "photographic universe", they would have been more likely to get the Kodak name into the social networks and gaming worlds. Basically, every decision that Kodak made was the worst possible business strategies of our time. They should have let a new generation of entrepreneurs step in and take charge of their digital world because they would have been prepared to take charge and drive the company into a new direction. This is a far cry from how Kodak spent its last few years of existence. The lesson learned here is that Kodak's challenges were not unique. If they did not have the attachment and weight of legacy, they could have moved into new ventures and been a force to be reckoned with. Instead, they choose to try to prolong the life of existing product lines while trying to create false synergies between the old and the new, and most of all they tried to base the strategy around obsolete users rather than creating a new business strategy that would fit with the future needs of the company. Kodak filed for bankruptcy in February of 2012.

If Kodak had the S.O.A.P. Framework, maybe the senior executives would have been able to see the tough decision that had to be made to save the company and not have to file for bankruptcy.

I want to give a couple of examples of some good, not really great, and poor strategies.

Santa heard my son Liam asking for a new bike for Christmas and, of course, I had to put it together. I am no tool junkie, but the one thing that I remember about my father is that all his tools were from Sears and they were Craftsman. I remember seeing the commercials about Craftsman tools and that they were the greatest things since sliced bread. I am not saying that Sears has a great business strategy because their stores are suffering now, but I feel that if they just sold tools they will be around longer. The strategy they have for their Craftsman tools is not that they are cool and easy to use, but that they will last virtually forever and they are guaranteed for life. For me I feel that this is a great business strategy to keep the high quality and guarantee for their tools.

On the flipside, Kitchen Aid was a company

that really was a mainstay in my house when I was a kid. My mother had a Kitchen Aid blender and virtually every attachment in the world and I swear that thing is still going strong today. Unfortunately, it is in my sister's house! Can you tell that I am a little upset over that one? Don't worry, one day I will get over it. This past year I went out and got Marisol, my wife, one because she was getting into cooking and it seemed like the perfect gift. We have had a couple of small problems so far, but nothing major. After I purchased the Kitchen Aid blender, I found out about the very poor strategy that their company started. Kitchen Aid decided to cut costs and save money on the way they made their mixers. Unfortunately, I did not go online and read any reviews because I was basing my purchase off the old strategy they had of high quality. But, things had changed and I felt it was a bad decision to cut the cost on production and the durability has taken a hit. This is a bad business strategy.

In the next chapter, I will discuss vendors and suppliers. I will go through the importance of reviewing contracts for discounts and picking new suppliers. I will apply the S.O.A.P. Framework to a contract issue I had with one of my suppliers and touch on inventory control.

Chapter 7

Building Relationships with Vendors

The one thing that I wished someone had taught me from the beginning is to interview and build a relationship with my vendors. This is a valuable lesson that I hope I can teach you now in your career. I want to tell a story of when I first opened Cedar Pharmacy in San Diego. After securing my location, I sat in my new office to get phone, Internet, and utilities set up. Then, I made calls to start getting suppliers for the office, backend and frontend of the pharmacy. What a fun task!

I want to tell you a quick story about my first experience with getting a medication wholesaler. First I called the big ones that I knew from working in the previous pharmacy positions. I called and set up 'meet and greets' with Cardinal and Amerisource Bergan (ABC). Wow! What a slap in the face. Cardinal was the first to come in. I was looking to use

Cardinal as my primary for medications and ABC for my medical supplies and durable medical equipment. Cardinal shows up thirty minutes late with no apology or anything, and after talking for about an hour they break out the paperwork. During the hour meeting we talked about my plans to have them as primary, what I was expecting to do in sales for a few months and what my opening order was going to be.

I'm not sure if you have ever done business with a medication wholesaler, but the paperwork makes buying a house look like second grade homework. I must have signed 500 pages, and it felt like I had given a pint of blood. We were starting to wrap up and were shaking hands; as the Cardinal rep walked out he turned to me and told me to have my $100,000 order ready by tomorrow and, by the way, I needed to order $50,000 per month. I was absolutely shocked because now I felt that he had not heard a word I said in the meeting. If you have started a business, you know that ordering $50,000 in inventory a month is suicide. I was only expecting to do maybe five to ten thousand in business for the first few months because it was going to take time to get people to change their minds about changing pharmacies. It would have been nice if he had told me this in the

CHAPTER 7 | BUILDING RELATIONSHIPS WITH VENDORS

beginning so we could have wrapped up the meeting three hours earlier. I got the same story from ABC, but at least he told me five minutes in what their rules were before we wasted each other's time with the mountain of forms that had to be filled out.

I had to change the way I attacked this so the next wholesaler was a mid-level company by the name of HD-Smith. I had met the sales rep previously at a convention so I had a bit of a relationship with him and my friend that owned a pharmacy in Los Angeles made the referral. I had a kind of comfort level before we talked so I felt like I was going to get a fair shake. The good thing was that they did not require a $50,000 per month spending spree. Their deal was to buy what you needed and pay every two weeks, and for my opening order, I had six months to pay it off. The terms were not as good, but at least I had a wholesaler. I know what you're thinking – that this is cool and the business can start.

The rep tells me not to worry about the opening order because they have a preset order that all the pharmacies do and are happy with. I figured, *"Hey, if all these pharmacies have done it, it must be good."* Plus, I felt we had a little bit of a relationship. He placed the order for me, and the meds were to be shipped in two weeks after I got my pharmacy license from the state. The day I was licensed and I called him up, and the medications were shipped the next day. I got to the pharmacy at 10 a.m., and about 30 minutes later the delivery truck showed up and brought a hand truck with eight totes of meds. I thought, *"Wow, only eight totes. This is awesome".* The delivery guy looked at me and smiled from ear to ear. He told me that he has 65 totes and with his hand truck he could only bring eight at a time. I almost crapped my pants. The total order he put in was for $423,763.87. That means I would have six months with free interest, but after that I would have one year to pay it off at 3 percent interest. That would make my payments around $35,000 a month. Not many businesses six months old can pay that kind of money and survive. I called him and told him to come and get the order. But, to my surprise, he told me that it was mine – *start selling*. The good thing is that it lit a fire under my butt to hustle and start selling.

The moral of my two stories here is that you need to double check, triple check and ask to triple check again before you sign a book of contracts. And, even if you get a referral to do business with someone, take the time to review and interview them thoroughly to build a solid trusting relationship. The old

Chapter 7 | Building Relationships with Vendors

saying that it is easier to sell something to a friend goes hand in hand with every part of the business life cycle. If you can build a trusting relationship with the vendor, I feel that it will change their agenda a bit and they will see that helping you grow your business the right way will help them grow their book of business.

Within this chapter, I will discuss the importance of building a relationship with all your vendors and the importance of reviewing contracts – not just in the beginning, but yearly – to help keep your focus on the growth of your business. I have reviewed contracts where the terms have changed after the auto renewal date and I was paying double percent on balances. This kind of stuff can really hurt a new or cash-strapped business. I will also apply the S.O.A.P. Framework to a problem that I encountered in one of my businesses and give examples of some clients issues and where it could have helped them to build a better relationship with their suppliers.

Vendor is from the French word *vendre* which means to sell. The definition that we all know is any person or company that sells goods or services to someone else in the economic production chain. This is such a cold impersonal definition, and we have this relationship with most of our vendors. This is what I would like for us to get away from and start building a relationship with all the vendors to help one another grow each other's book of business.

I want to tell you a couple of stories: one about a great relationship with a vendor and one about a casual relationship with a vendor. First, the casual relationship, and where it went wrong. I worked with my client, and he purchased a medical clinic in San Diego and slowly converted it into a medical day spa. With that conversion, he started changing some of the companies he purchased supplies from. One of the companies was a referral that I had given him because a near and dear friend of mine that worked in their public relations department. My thoughts were that the sales rep would not want to let down a fellow employee and he would work even harder to ensure we had all the tools necessary to succeed. When I say "our success", I mean the success of the medical spa and the success of the sales person. The more he helps educate his clients on how to sell the products, the more products we buy. I do not blame the sales guy 100 percent. I feel that we should take the blame 50-50. On our side, we did not take the time to really get to know the sales guy and figure out what made him tick. Finding what motivates a salesperson besides sales can help build a trustworthy and focused relationship. Going back to relationship building with your vendors is key. Learning more about him as a person would have helped us gain insight and built that relationship where he would want to make sure that we had everything we needed to get from point A to point B.

The issue we had was that there was a marketing planogram available with specific products and marketing opportunities that have been proven to work in the medical day spa world. We would order the products, and a planogram (visual representation of a store's shelf layout) was supposed to accompany them, but they never did. Well, when I went to the salesperson to ask about my planogram, he turned into the "yes man" and not the "let's take action man." He did not take our wants and needs seriously. He was already making money off of us because we were selling the products and he was meeting his sales quota with his company. But what he didn't realize is that we could have been selling three times that amount if he would have taken the time to help us setup the marketing and planograms properly. After many attempts to get the marketing materials, I decided to go over his head and call the company. Guess what? I got some of the same treatment. I started thinking that this was a mistake going with this company, and my client was upset with me for referring him to a place that did not respect the business relationship.

The products were awesome, and I felt obligated to continue since my friend worked there and referred me to them in the first place. It took me a bit to realize that the reason we were not getting anywhere is because they were getting what they needed and did not care if the medical spa got theirs. I suggested to Martin that we cut the orders. Before we did that I called my friend in the PR department and asked her what the guy's deal was, if we had done anything to damage the relationship. To the best of her knowledge, things were great and everyone was happy. After speaking with her, we went to the sales guy and tried to understand why we were not getting the materials that other medical spas in the area were getting.

We contacted another spa in the area that also purchased products from the vendor, and they said, "If you don't stay on top of him, you will never get anything from him in the way of marketing materials and planograms." To me that is frustrating because I am all about providing customer service. That is why I think the whole salesperson payment schedule should be changed, but that is something I will discuss in the sales chapter. The good thing is that after some effort on our part, we were able to get the sales guy to come down about 30 percent. That 30 percent is better than the zero percent we were getting, but the road is long and hard, and we will crack him. In a nice way, of course!

The great relationship was with McKesson Drug. McKesson was my one of my wholesalers for the pharmacy that did not make me jump through hoops just to be a client. The reason is because the salesperson Bridgette and I hit if off and became "work friends." Over the years we became real friends and we still talk and meet for lunch. The benefit of having Bridgette was that any new programs or products that were coming out, I found out about them ahead of time. We discussed any new contract issues or renewals and any discounts as a result of an increase in purchasing volume. This was a benefit for the both of us because I was less likely to cheat on her and purchase from another vendor. The benefit for her was that she had a strong store that kept growing, and purchases were climbing, which meant that her bonuses and commissions were growing. This was the classic "I scratch your back, you scratch mine" scenario.

The bad thing is that after Bridgette left McKesson my relationship with them soon fell apart. The new guy tried, but to no avail. This was a relationship that we used the S.O.A.P. Framework on, so I will use this as my example.

Subjective

The problem was that since Bridgette left there was little to no customer service, and when I needed something the new sales guy was nowhere to be found.

The problem started when I purchased another store and we were supposed to get a volume discount, marketing materials, updated website, and other odds and ends to help make the transition into the new business easier and better. In the S.O.A.P Framework example, I am just going to focus on the volume discount. As time went on and the discount was not applied, I was getting worried about getting a refund from the accounting department at McKesson because over the years they had been slow to offer, even with Bridgette fighting for me. The aggravating part of this was that the sales guy (we will call him Tom) would promise a mountain and only deliver a grain of sand.

When I looked at this problem, I found it to be a breakdown in all three aspects of the additional conditions. Physical-the computer software system provided by McKesson had the discount loaded but not active. Human-no one at the accounting division activated the discount and the Tom failed to follow up on behalf of his client. Organizational-- the policies and procedures established by the wholesaler were not being followed, there were no policies and procedures for this problem or Tom and his boss just did not care because the volume we were giving them is what they wanted and needed to reach their bonuses. Most salespeople only want to reach their numbers to make their bosses happy. I had multiple meeting and calls to try rectifying the problem, but it took over a year and a few lawyers to get it done.

Objective

When you order medications from McKesson, an invoice comes with every order with a discount code and column that signifies your discount. Mine was blank. In the system it showed, but not on the invoices. This was a big deal because I earned it; we liked to pass the savings on to our customers and it improved cash flow. The customers never

S.O.A.P. Framework

knew when we were getting discounts but they always enjoyed them when we gave them, and we liked to surprise the clients because it built buzz and a better following of loyal clientele. I am going to use a part of framework I developed named the Five W's.

1. What is causing the problem?

    a. McKesson failing to apply the volume discount.

2. What is being affected?

    a. The pharmacy bottom line.

    b. The customers of the pharmacy because they are not benefiting from the savings.

    c. McKesson because they will lose a client.

    d. The staff of the pharmacy because cash flow is not as robust, so that means fewer raises and other bonuses.

3. What is the impact of this problem on the business?

    a. Loss of customers to competitors with better pricing.

    b. Cost to find another wholesaler

c. Payroll to update the system for all the new manufacturers of the medications. My pharmacies carry anywhere from $250,000 to $600,000 in inventory. Updating all those NDCs was very costly.

d. Cash flow

e. This problem took me away from growing the business for over a month. The lost revenue was big.

4. What inputs do I need to solve the problem?

    a. Get the management team at McKesson to understand that if they are going to offer a discount then they should hold up their end of the bargain.

    b. Need to get a better understanding of the policies and procedures for how and when the discounts should have occurred.

    c. Find a way to motivate Tom to do his job.

5. What are the limitations that will impact the solution for success of this problem?

    a. Not being able to discuss this with the accounting team.

b. Not being able to speak with Tom on a regular basis because he failed to answer his phone.

   c. Not being able to speak with Tom's boss for the same reason.

   d. Even if I were able to speak with the accounting department, how long would it take them to cut the rebate check?

   e. Limited budget to hire legal to go after them.

Assessment

After identifying the problem and evaluating the data, it was time to come up with a couple of solutions to try to get this issue solved.

1. Set a meeting in person with Tom.

2. Set a meeting in person with Tom and his boss.

3. Hire an attorney.

4. Stop paying our bill until they paid up on the discount.

5. Switch wholesalers to try to gain leverage.

6. Find out if the problem was a software issue.

7. Cry!

Plan

It was time to evaluate our proposed solutions and pick the one that we felt was going to work best. Unfortunately, the one we picked was not advantageous to either party. We chose to stop paying our bill to get their attention. It worked, and the next day Tom and his boss were in the pharmacy demanding payment. This led to a big fight which resulted in us not getting the discount we were owed. Apparently, part of the contract included a default clause which meant if we defaulted on our payment, then any discounts we were promised became null and void. Next, our customers became upset because we had to change wholesalers and this caused a delay in the delivery of their medications. Instead of getting our normal delivery the next day, it was taking a couple of days. Luckily, this only lasted about a week. Even though this solution did not work with McKesson, it opened the door for us to do business with a brand new wholesaler called Cardinal Drug. We went into those negotiations locked and loaded, full of questions and addendums for our contract with each other. I am happy to say that everything turned out for the better with the new wholesaler, our customers, the pharmacy, and Cardinal Drug. We were both excited to move forward with this new relationship and a new chapter in our pharmacy life.

Having a great relationship with the people you do business with is a win-win for both of you. You can gain insight into the company you're doing business with because the salesperson will open up to you for trust reasons. When there is a problem or question that needs to get answered, your rep will go to bat for you and get you what you need in a timely fashion. Even when things are going great having that trusting relationship and knowing that things are going to run smoothly with your vendors saves you time, money and in my case hair because you have less stress about the store getting its supplies and it will gives you more time to grow the business.

In the next chapter, I am going to discuss the importance of knowing what the numbers mean to you and the success of your business. Some of the parts I will discuss are the importance of cash flow to sales, why the profit margin is important for you to focus on, and a basic overall understanding of what the numbers mean and why you need to know them to understand if you have a viable business or not.

Chapter 8

Tracking Numbers

One of the things that I felt gave me a great advantage was that I tracked the numbers on an Excel spreadsheet from the beginning of my business and I was on top of them daily. Tracking the numbers on paper in the beginning gives you an intimate feel for the business. This was important to me because I could see issues much faster and I could take action to fix them before they became a problem. I used QuickBooks, but it was so impersonal for me. I felt the spreadsheet was the key to knowing where I stood in my business.

Was I viable or not? It gave me a real-time snapshot so I could make decisions faster and easier. Understanding where the numbers are coming from and what they mean can greatly increase your chances of success. By tracking the numbers in Excel and building spreadsheets, it helped me gain a sense of connection with the numbers. Ultimately, you do not run the business. The numbers do. If you are opening a business, I am assuming that your goal is to make money. I know that I wanted to be profitable within my first year of opening. By understanding what the numbers are saying, you should be able to learn how to make money the most efficient way possible. If you are opening your business today, then start tracking the numbers today. If you already have a business established, then start now. Don't let your accountant make a profit and loss sheet or balance sheet for you. Make it yourself and look at what it is telling you.

I had a friend that called me to review his medical practice because he was seeing tons of patients weekly, but was still struggling with cash flow. He felt that he needed to see more patients.

I said, "Hold on. Let's talk first and then figure out where and what you need to do next." Michael realized that he was having a problem when his office manager came to him and said that there was not enough money to pay the bills and she could not figure out why. She felt that all the insurance companies were paying on time and that the patients were paying their co-pays, but still there was no cash. Michael knew the average cost it took him to see a patient and the income from that patient. By doing the simple math he figured that he needed another $3,000 per month, so that would equate to six to eight more patients per week. He was focused on selling. But, getting more patients was going to cost more money, and that was something he did not have at the time. I told him, "Let's look at the numbers to see what is happening in the practice."

A couple of possible issues were that he was not making enough gross profit per patient to cover the bills and expenses, the insurances were not paying or someone else was pocketing the cash. Let's tackle each issue starting with profit per patient. He felt that his profit per patient was right around $75. After further review that was for his cash patients, but his insurance patients' average was only $35. Why was the average so different? Were all the insurances paying the same amount? Was he charging for all the services that he provided to the patient on that day? Were some patients not being charged at all? He could not answer these questions because he only had lump sum numbers. They were not broken down into groups because his accountant and bookkeeper only did the gross numbers for tax purposes.

I had him go back and track three months' worth of patients and break them down into cash, each type of insurance that he took, and no-pay patients. After reviewing the numbers, I could see that there were way too many no-pays. The cash patients that did pay were his best option, but a good portion of the insurance reimbursements were horrible. He had four or five that had not paid him in months, and some were only paying him five to ten dollars per patient per visit. The worst part is that the biller did not bill for all the services that he provided to the patient on that visit. Basically, he was losing money on two-thirds of the patients he was seeing. He did not need more sales. He needed to track the numbers better and get reimbursed for the services rendered.

I sent him a spreadsheet that had him track the number of patients and gross margin for each kind of patient. I also had him write down total sales, cost of goods, expenses, gross profit, and gross margin for the month and for the year. This exercise took him at most 30 minutes a month, and it helped him see where the numbers were taking the practice at a glance. This was a revelation for him, because now he could see where the money was or was not and what it took to make money in his business. Granted, he is not a businessman. He is a doctor and a damn good one, but these were things you need to know before you get wiped out. The good thing is that no one was stealing from him except for the insurance companies that were not paying on time. With a couple of phone calls and some threats, most of the insurance companies paid up.

I told him to go through each insurance contract and renegotiate it. If they did not budge, drop them. The cost to keep low margin patients was a drag on his business. If he did not want to drop that plan because he had patients that he loved, then he should have changed his procedures with those plans. Spend less time with the patient or get a nurse practitioner or physician's assistant to see them and the last part was to raise his cash prices to make up the difference from the insurance company downfall. To my surprise, he did a bit of everything I suggested. He kept the low margin patients, but changed the procedures in the office to cut down on expenses with those patients. I thought that this was a great idea because it helped him build relationships that ultimately helped him grow into another office. Once he figured out the meaning of the numbers, he was able to turn his attention to growing a profitable practice.

After he took the blinders off and had the

chance to see the numbers and understand them, he was able to make decisions based on performance, not just guessing. He was operating on the basis that his accountant, office manager and biller knew what he wanted out of the business. The office manager and biller are good at their jobs, but they are not entrepreneurs and do not really know what the numbers mean. As far as the accountant goes, they are basically a historian of numbers. They can tell you how the business has performed in the past, but they can't tell how it is going to perform in the future. Only you, the entrepreneur, can do that because only you can change the direction of the company.

If you start collecting the data from the beginning, you can track your gross margin. One of the big numbers that you want to focus on is having a high gross margin because that translates into high gross profit. That is the cash cow that feeds your business. I want to be clear that I don't want you obsessing over the numbers every time one of them drops or rises. I just want you to know what the numbers mean so you can move and take the necessary action when there are shifts in the growth or decline of your business.

CHAPTER 8 | TRACKING NUMBERS

Being an entrepreneur is being a student of your business. Learning what the numbers mean will arm you with the knowledge to catch the business before it falls or grow it when the time is right. Now that Michael has taken the time to learn the numbers, he has taken his practice to a new level. He is actually seeing fewer patients by choice, but making more money. Learning the numbers and not relying on his accountant, office manager or biller was the best business decision he has made because it allowed him to fix a problem before it got too far out of hand and kept him from making a bigger mistake in trying to go after more sales when that is not what he needed. It is important to remember that every business is a living, breathing entity. Your best chance of success lies in monitoring crucial numbers and knowing when to give them the attention they deserve before things get too far out of hand.

We have all heard that cash is *king*. It's true! Companies that focus and live on sales and profits will die on sales and profits if cash flow is not positive. Not having positive cash flow in times of recession is a critical factor in the success of the business. An example is a client that has a construction company. If he links the cost to the time when the houses are done and ready for purchase and ignores the cash outflow it takes to build the house, he might run out of cash before the house is sold. When times are good he can dip into the overdraft to make up any cash shortfalls. When times are tough and he has to rely on the banks to keep him cash happy, this is very risky. He needs to manage all of the finances well enough to avoid the danger of negative cash flow. As a young entrepreneur, he did focus solely on the sales and fell into a money pit. After spending some time together and learning what the numbers mean, he now has a strong grasp of them. He also has the confidence to make bold moves in cash strong times and pull back when business is weak.

For the young entrepreneurs out there that might be reading this book, let me give a few definitions of some of the key numbers that you need to follow in your business. Profit is defined as the difference between the amount earned and the amount spent in buying, operating, or producing a product. Cash flow is the total amount of money being moved into and out of a business. Sales are the transaction between two parties for some type of payment. Gross margin is the total sales revenue minus the cost of goods sold, divided by the total sales revenue and is expressed as a percentage. The gross margin represents the percent of total sales revenue that the company retains after incurring the direct costs associated with producing the goods and services sold by a company.

The higher the percentage, the more cash is retained on each dollar of sales to service its other costs and obligations. The last couple of terms I would like to define for you are *assets*. There are fixed assets that are long-term benefits that the company will have for more than one year, like land or equipment. Current assets are those that will be used in less than one year like cash, inventory or accounts receivable. The last term is *expenses* and they are fixed, variable, accrued and operational. These are costs that a business incurs through its operations. Now that the Bernard's Dictionary part is over with, let's move on. As a young entrepreneur that did not get an MBA, knowing these terms would have given me a head start. That is why I am happy to share with other young entrepreneurs out there striving towards their dreams of owning a viable business in today's competitive world.

For my S.O.A.P. Framework example in this chapter, I am going to apply it to growth. When can you and when do you know when to expand your business? I went through this issue when we wanted to expand our sausage business from the brick and mortar to farmer's markets to get more exposure and hopefully build contacts with other local venders for meat and veggies. I realize that I just dropped a bomb about our sausage business. My wife and I opened a chorizo sausage business in 2010 and sold it in 2013. It was a great ride, and we enjoyed digging into something that was outside our comfort zone.

Subjective

Here we wanted to take the chorizo from our plant and café and start selling it in farmer's markets. The plans were to open one market, build a following, earn a profit, and then expand one market about every two months, if the requirements were met. We had two issues that needed to be handled. The first was the plan for growth, and the second was our partner we took on to work in the farmer's markets. We will call the partner Steve.

I laid out a plan to start one market and slowly expand into another market about every two months if we reached our sales and *cash flow goals*. Unfortunately, our partner Steve had his own agenda. He played games by causing problems between Marisol and

I to distract us from the business. His plan was to use our resources to sell his products and not promote the business as a whole. He would not follow the pricing plans or any of the procedures we set up in our team meetings. This problem was both human and organizational. It was *Human* because we did not do a thorough enough background check on our new partner. It was *Organizational* because we needed tighter policies and better controls over what all of our employees and partners do when working outside the plant and café.

Objective

We knew there was a problem when he was having meeting with new markets behind our back and telling us after the fact. He had the "I will deal with the consequences later" attitude. More problems started when the employees complaining about his attitude when neither Marisol or I were not there, his unauthorized meetings, purchasing equipment without authorization and signing contracts with farmer's markets without having staff, product, or any infrastructure whatsoever. I am going to use my *5 Whats* for this issue.

1. What is causing the problem?

a. Steve undermining our authority.

b. Planning for growth without having a pathway to follow.

2. What is being affected?

    a. Cash flow

    b. Employees were upset because they were not getting trained properly or paid correctly.

    c. We did not have the set cost to open one market up so we were never able to get a true cost analysis.

    d. Had no idea how long it would take to be profitable.

    e. What did our gross margin need to be?

    f. How much overhead did we have to add?

    g. Customer service lacked because no set policies were written.

3. What is the impact of this problem on the business?

    a. Loss of customers.

    b. Loss of quality employees.

      c. Tension in the workplace between everyone.

      d. Put the company in a cash flow crunch so I had to borrow money from the pharmacy to keep this afloat.

      e. Cash flow

      f. The problem took our focus off the main store and its growth, which hurt the overall business.

4. What inputs do I need to solve the problem?

      a. Needed better communication between Steve, Marisol and I.

      b. Needed to have stronger ground rules instead allowing him to wing it and almost bring us down.

      c. Needed to take the time to build out a plan from the cash flow standpoint to set up a growth plan.

5. What are the limitations that will impact the solution for success of this problem?

      a. Lack of communication.

      b. Lack of plan.

c. Having a partner that wanted to do his own thing.

   d. Lack of cash flow due to mistakes made in expansion.

Assessment

With all the data, we needed to come up with a plan that would save the business and salvage the relationship between Marisol, Steve and I.

1. Establish a small business plan to get us back on track.

2. Cut markets until we get back on our feet.

3. Cut ties with Steve.

4. Sell the business.

Plan

We actually tried to do a step-by-step plan to keep the business going. The first thing we did was to cut markets and save cash. Then I wrote out a financial page to show how we can make this happen. On the financial page, I took the gross sales of one of the markets and drew it up like this so he could understand that the money has to come from somewhere. The average farmer's market would do $100,000 in sales over the next year. We had a gross margin of 40 percent. Then we would have an added expense cost of $10,000 for the year for rent, commissions, bookkeeping and other goodies to run the business. The nice thing is that our receivables were less than a week. Here is how it is done. Start by figuring out your cost of goods (COGS) on the new business, which is what it will cost to set up a market and stock it with product. Since our margin is 40 percent of sales, the COGS are at 60 percent or $60,000. Then, you're going to add the overhead expense of $10,000 to the $60,000 to get what we would need to handle a market that was producing $100,000 in revenue per year. Then, you take the total money needed to produce those sales and divide it by the number of days in the period you're trying to cover, which is one year or 365 days, and we had a daily cost of $192 to pay for that market. Next, take the daily number and multiply it by the days for collection. In our case, it only took seven day to collect. With this calculation you can get a rough idea of the cash needed to operate that market and any new market we wanted to open. The cash needed was about $1,400. I establish a money line that said once we get double that then we can expand because it will not hurt the core business. You must always protect the core business.

The big problem was with Steve. He was stealing and lying about the money being made at the farmer's markets he was controlling. The icing on the cake is that we all agreed to the plan I put together, but he was still trying to do his own thing. You cannot have a partner that has a different agenda than you or the business does. So we cut ties with him, and afterwards Marisol and I really felt that this business was taking away from her being the greatest mom in the world, so we sold the business and I am happy to say that Marisol is super happy, the guy we sold to is super happy and you know what they say about "happy wife, happy life." Even I have had a bounce in my step.

The benefits of using S.O.A.P Framework on this problem was that we were able to somewhat reel in our renegade partner, but most importantly we were able to truly establish a true cost for opening a market and what it would take to keep it going and not hurt the core business. Having this happen to us helped us change our focus on how we handled a partner that nearly took us down.

It also gave Marisol and I a chance to work as a team outside the family setting. In this instance, the S.O.A.P Framework did more for my family life than my business life.

Knowing what the numbers mean makes it easier to make a move to solve a problem in cash flow, like Dr. Michael did in the first example I gave in this chapter and, change pricing or looking for opportunities to grow like we did with the farmers markets. I wanted to give a couple more examples of why it's important to focus on your financial management. There was a plastic bottling company that contacted me about a new sales opportunity. They were contacted by a Florida company that was looking to purchase $30,000 in bottles for a new skincare product. They called me to help them figure out how much cash they would need to produce the bottles, when they would see a return on the new business and if it would be worth it for them to take on the new business. After a short financial discussion, we figured that it was going to cost them $20,000 to produce the bottles. It was going to take six weeks to make the bottles; at that time they could invoice for the products and have a 30-day collection period, which would put the company in a negative hole for 10 to 11 weeks. We talked about the cash flow they had and if they could handle that much cash gone for 10 to 11 weeks before seeing a payment. They could, and it ended up being a great deal for them because they were able to make $10,000 profit and since then the Florida company has reordered three more times.

Another piece to the numbers puzzle is knowing the prices. When do you raise them and what happens if you don't? I learned this early on in my pharmacy career because Merck, one the largest drug companies in the world, would raise their prices about 4% every quarter. Because they raised theirs, I had to raise mine, and it was easy for me to explain this to the customers because it was public information. But when I had to raise them for other reasons (like maintaining the gross profit I wanted or hiring a new employee or general cost of living increases), it was a little harder to explain.

Here is a big doozy! Most of my businesses I have started from scratch. Yet, among the few that I have purchased, there was one that had not raised the prices in over five years. Even though I did work in the pharmacy for a few weeks, I was so focused on contracts, employees, and customers that I over looked product and service pricing. Buying this pharmacy was a challenge from day one for many reasons, but after I got there and started working I soon realized that this pharmacy was not making enough money to survive in the long run. The financials that were given to me were, let's just say that the rules of accounting were *ignored*. I am not going to go off on a big tangent, but if you're buying a business, beware of fraudulent business accounting practices. Just to show you that it can happen to anyone, here are a couple examples: Enron, ERA mining (a company that Caterpillar purchased in 2012) and the Halifax Bank of Scotland, just to name a few high-profile accounting errors, to put it mildly. OK, now back to the pricing. The pharmacy had not raised their prices in over five years so I had to raise them and raise them quickly. I knew that I would lose some customers, but hopefully I could gain a few with my marketing campaign and it would offset the loss. It was not a cool thing to do and I hate doing it, but I had to raise the prices by 40 percent.

Customers asked, "Why such big price changes? Why raise them all at once?" And I was honest with the customers and told them that if I was to stay in business I had to raise the prices to meet current market demands. After the first initial shock of the huge price increases, I was able to raise prices on a quarterly basis at much smaller increments that most of the customers did not even notice. You have to raise prices. If you don't, then your profit margins will shrink because your COGS and cost of living are climbing. These are called *creeping expenses*. You have to keep an eye on the creeps or they will rob you blind. That is what I used to tell my salespeople when they wanted to sell products at a gross margin that was outside of our normal discounts.

In the next chapter, I am going to discuss sales. I will review the importance of sales, how to get them, and how to know if the sale is good or bad. The last thing to discuss will be what I did to train my sales staff to work as a team and not as individual units trying to reach sales goals. I will also debate the difference between giving a salesperson a salary compared to commission and the impact it had on my business.

CHAPTER 9

Improving the Sales Process with S.O.A.P.

Earlier in this book, I said that sales are not the important thing to track in the business. Now, let me add a couple of clarifying statements. Sales are not the most important number to track; *gross margin and cash flow are*, because that is what makes a business viable. BUT, (and that is a big but) you will need sales to be able to have gross margin and cash flow to track. You will need good, high-quality sales to be a strong company and very good gross margins and cash flow to be a viable company. Tracking the sales numbers *only* is a big mistake that many new entrepreneurs make early on in their businesses. I made that mistake too early in my career. It wasn't until I opened Cedar Pharmacy that I learned what the important numbers were to track to see if I was going to make it or not. At first, I only looked at the daily sales, and as they grew, I felt that

I was moving in the right direction. Early on I had a scare because I was not able to pay my medication bill to H-D Smith. I sat back and looked at the sales numbers, and they were great. For being a pharmacy that was less than a year old, I was doing $30,000 a month in sales and I figured that there was no way I did not have enough cash to pay my bills. Then, I soon realized that I had to get quality sales to maintain the gross margin I needed to stay alive.

After I settled into the mindset of getting quality sales, I had to develop a plan to figure out where they were and how to get them. When I first started I just knew that people were going to be pouring in to get their meds, and when that did not happen I changed the mindset to go and get as many sales as I could by changing my marketing plan. The one thing that I missed was to qualify the sales to maintain the gross margins I needed to be viable.

The first step I took in my new sales plan was to build my confidence in asking for the sale. I was deathly afraid of going up to a stranger and asking the important questions to see if they would be a good fit for my pharmacy. At first I thought that it took nerve to go get a sale, but the only time you need nerve is when you're afraid of being rejected. So I developed the "no fear, no expectations" attitude and starting asking all the doctors in the building the questions I needed to get to know them and qualify them as a client for my pharmacy. I also changed my thought process from the "you don't ask you don't get" theory to "give great value and they will want to get." Soon after my approach changed, the doctors saw the confidence I had in my abilities and they started trusting me and started sending patients to the pharmacy. This was step one of many to build a customer base that would make Steve Jobs proud.

The next thing I had to work on was my niche. Why would doctors want to send patients to my pharmacy over any other, and why would patients want to change from their current pharmacy to come to mine? I mean, everyone promises great service and excellent products. In the case of my pharmacy all the products were the exact same as the competition. The niche that I developed was convenience. We handled all the insurance problems for the doctors, so it saved them time and money. Being able to provide a service to a busy doctor (and with the crappy reimbursement from the insurance companies nowadays) was huge for them. They jumped all over it. As for the patients I provided them with easy fax prescriptions and pickup or delivery of the medications to their office or home. This service allowed the patients to fax their script to us and we would get it ready before they came by so there was no wait or if they did not have time to come by we would deliver the meds to them. They loved the service because none of the chain stores offered that service. Now with the added extra service I could keep my prices a little higher and maintain the margins I needed to be viable.

The next thing I did was to add employees that spoke the language of the area. This provided customers that did not speak English well or not at all a comfort level that they did not get elsewhere. These three simple little changes increased my sales from $30,000 a month to $73,000 a month in less than three months. This was a great start, but now if I was to reach my goal of breaking $10 million a year in revenue I had to start really building the business.

The strategies that I used to increase sales in my pharmacy are easy to adapt to any business. Understanding how to qualify clients and build a niche is all part of the process to lead your business to the next level. For me the next level was to focus on the intermediate goals with maintaining the overall focus on reaching annual revenue of $10 million. In "The E-Myth," Gerber talked about how very few small businesses will even reach a million (much less ten million). Now the challenge was on. I had to prove to myself that I could be better that the average business. I hope that after you read my book it will challenge you to handle your problem solving and growth a little differently and shoot for the goals that are just outside of your comfort level. In the last chapter I will talk about reaching for that potential and stepping outside the areas of comfort and how it will help you grow and beat down the fear that most people have when it comes to doing something different and new.

Running your business, the one thing that you absolutely need is sales. If you cannot generate sales then you will not be able to reach viability in the business. Now to qualify that statement a little more, not all sales are treated equally. There are the good, the bad and the ugly. The problem is that 99 percent of salespeople think that all sales are good, and I know that this is a difficult concept for salespeople to understand. They are not all good. I don't blame them because they have been taught to reach sales goals and only to focus on the sales numbers. The other part that has been engrained in their heads is that any sale is a good sale and the bigger the better. In fact, the least important thing is the size of the sale. The most important part of the sale is the amount of gross profit you are earning from it. Many entrepreneurs who do not heed this information will soon be out of business.

Not too long ago I met with a young man starting a new long-term care pharmacy, and his mindset was to find the largest homes and go after them. He felt that his company was well equipped to handle everything. He had a great facility, all the proper marketing and advertising, well trained salespeople and enough confidence to take down Thor. His mindset was that small clients were just a waste of time and more expensive to deal with than the larger clients and the larger the client the faster he would reach his sales goals. To me growing a business from the ground up is what gets me out of bed every day, and the focus and determination to grow and be successful is what drives me. My advice to him was to sign up all the small homes he could find and only go after a couple of the bigger ones in the beginning. The reason behind my thinking is twofold. If you only have two or three large homes and one leaves you for whatever reason, then a large chunk of your business is now gone. If one of the small homes leaves you, then the percent lost is small and easily overcome.

A solid customer base is the key to success in any business, but smaller customers are the backbone of most companies because they pay a little more for the services because they don't have the volume to get bigger discounts. It is easier to maintain gross margins and profit with smaller clients than larger ones. My goal was to have a 10 to 1 ratio of small homes to large homes. Each of the small homes would generate $10,000 per month and require a third of the labor hours to maintain it compared to the larger home that would generate $60,000 per month but require triple the labor and large volume discounts. On the smaller homes I did not overcharge them, but they did pay a premium until they reached a level of sales or if they signed a long-term contract then I would extend a better discount for them. Having a strong smaller client base in your company will strengthen your company's margins.

As I mentioned earlier, smaller clients are the backbone of your company. The reason why is that as long as you treat smaller clients with love and respect they will be loyal to you forever. There are very few people in this world that will change their habits. Most of us hate it and so do businesses. When they are happy and comfortable they will stay. On the flipside, larger companies can be pulled away by competition for the simple explanation of price. Their margins are tight already and if they can get cheaper service elsewhere, then they will up and leave you the second your contract expires. In my long-term care pharmacy (LTC) I focused on the smaller homes because the cost and time to sign them was thirty minutes and a lunch for the staff of five to ten. Where going after a larger client, the time was tripled and the cost was considerably higher.

The last point is that smaller clients add stability to your company. A key point that my banker Nino from First Republic Bank taught me is that to get a loan or any kind of financing, they would want to see a list of my business accounts. They are looking to see how many of the accounts are more than 30 percent of your businesses. If you had two large clients that equaled 60 percent of your business the less likely the bank will loan you money. Because if one of the large clients leaves your business then how are you going to pay the loan back? Plus the larger clients have more control of your time. If they need something they will expect you to supply it ASAP.

CHAPTER 9 | IMPROVING THE SALES PROCESS WITH S.O.A.P.

I had a large hospice care client that would call me at 2 a.m., and I had to get up and drive thirty minutes to my pharmacy to fill a prescription. At that point I had a decision to make: Should I call my delivery guy to come and take it or just do it myself? If I called him then I had to wait for him to get there and pay the extra after-hours fee to him or take my sleep time away and deliver it myself. Because of time and cost I normally just did it myself. My smaller clients were more efficient and called during regular business hours to get emergency meds pre-stocked where the larger client did not have as tight controls with their policies and procedures. The other not so great thing with larger clients is that they would dictate the price because of the sheer volume of business they were giving. So the gross margin with large homes was 19 percent compared to 32 percent with small homes. Don't get me wrong: Once you get to a certain point, larger companies will help get you to the next level. They are a key component in the ladder, just not the main component.

Here in San Diego there are three main LTC pharmacies, and one was the big monster that we all feared because they were dirty. They would go and talk trash about the other pharmacies or they would bully the homes into switching. In the beginning I had a problem with that but I soon realized that if you conduct your business sales with honestly and integrity, the homes will either never leave or come back as soon as they realized the grass is not always greener on the other side. As you know, most of the time it is just smellier.

Most people tie sales and marketing together. Yes, you need them to work hand in hand, but they need their separate attention. Now the technical definition of sales is the activity of a business where you are engaged in selling a product or service for profit. To me, sales are not only a process, but an extension of your brand. When a salesperson leaves to go out and sell a product or service that I have developed, they need to sell it like I would. They need to have the same passion for selling that product that I would, and if they don't then they are not a good fit for my company. The one type of employee that I have gone through more of are salespeople. But I have developed a plan to my hiring of salespeople and how I like them to work, which helps tie all the pieces of the sales process together with all the parts of the business that sales touch.

I want to apply the S.O.A.P. Framework

to a problem I had with my salespeople. While starting the LTC Pharmacy, one of the problems that plagued me was how to pay the salespeople. They would fight over territories and cause troubles for the other areas of the business because the internal competition within the sales department. I had to figure out a way to make all the salespeople work with each other to complement their sales skills as well as compensate them to where they would work hard to ensure the company's success.

Subjective

The onset of the issue was right after I hired my first salesperson. In the beginning, my sales department was my office manager/part-time sales person, Debbie, and myself. Debbie went out twice a week to call on new homes and visit existing business and I handled mostly new business. She went out and pitched the pharmacy and our services to new homes in the area. She was starting to get busy with office stuff, so I decided to hire another person, Melissa, to come in and be part of the sales team. She was well qualified and fairly mild-mannered, but very aggressive and a damn good salesperson once she was in front of a client. I went on a couple sales calls with her, and she impressed me, so I offered her the job.

My problems started with Melissa when she crossed the line by trying to steal business from Debbie. I am a firm believer in allowing the employees to work out their differences on their own and if they can't, then I would step in and help. At first, Debbie told me not to worry about it, that she and Melissa would work it out. At that point, I put it on the back burner and moved on with my work.

Some of the additional contributing factors were human and organizational elements. The human element was that Melissa had disregard for the boundaries that I had outlined for the territories and she was over the top with greed. I have no problem with being money-motivated but it is important to be respectful of the business and other employees. The organizational part was that I needed to establish a better sales training guide and protocols.

Objective

After I received a couple of phone calls from the homes that we were already servicing and they were unhappy with Melissa's selling techniques. This was a problem that I knew I needed to address

Chapter 9 | Improving the Sales Process with S.O.A.P.

immediately. I needed to find a happy medium with Debbie, Melissa and the rest of my staff so we could work as one big happy family.

The last straw for me was when I received a call from my most loyal nursing home and they were not happy with our service. This problem required me to take time to really think through the entire sales process and not make any snap decisions.

1. What is causing the problem?

    a. Melissa being too aggressive with her sales approach.

    b. Debbie not being more assertive with teaching the sales process to Melissa.

    c. Dr. Gram by not spending more time training and having a formal sales manual.

2. What is being affected?

    a. Relationships between coworkers.

    b. Cash flow.

    c. Melissa's work performance.

    d. Debbie's work performance.

S.O.A.P. Framework

    e. The overall flow of how the products left the pharmacy and were delivered to the homes.

    f. Inventory.

    g. Payroll.

    h. The complaints from the nursing homes.

3. What is the impact of this problem on the business?

    a. Loss of customers.

    b. Unhappy managers at the LTC homes.

    c. Tension in the workplace between everyone.

    d. Cash flow.

    e. The problem took our focus off the main store and its growth, which hurt the overall business.

4. What inputs do I need to solve the problem?

    a. The managers at the homes.

    b. Debbie the office manager.

c. Melissa the salesperson.

d. The accountant and inventory staff.

5. What are the limitations that will impact the solution for success of this problem?

    a. Melissa's willingness to change.

    b. The staff willing to give Melissa another chance.

    c. Building the trust back with the homes.

    d. Repair the reputation of the pharmacy.

    e. Failure to develop a better compensation plan.

    f. Failure to develop a better training guide.

    g. Need to establish hiring ground rules.

Assessment

The problem boiled down to Melissa being more aggressive to get any sales she could because her goal was to make as much money as possible. The commission basis point system forced her to step outside the boundaries and make her own rules to ensure she had the highest sales and the biggest paycheck. This affected everyone in the chain from the production, accounting, office manager, sales department and most importantly the client. The things that I had to accomplish here was to establish a pay system that would make it fair for everyone and keep a good salesperson on staff. I had to establish a new set of guidelines and training so this would not happen again.

Possible solutions

1. Fire Melissa.

2. Write new guidelines for sales training.

3. Establish new guidelines for hiring sales personnel.

4. Alter the pay structure.

5. Accompany Melissa to all sales calls until she earns my trust back.

6. Fire Debbie because she is too soft as an office manager.

Plan

I choose to alter the pay structure because this would control Melissa's urge to overtake the other employees. After, I would establish stronger sales training for all current and new hires.

By changing the pay structure and building a new training guide I figured this would put an end to any further competition issues. After I built the new system I put Debbie in charge of making sure it worked and everyone followed it to a "T". The risk was that the salesperson would not understand how the new pay structure would work and how it would benefit all parties involved. It protected the employees when they had a down month and protected the company because it took all the external bull crap out of the picture. The follow-up policy I started was to call the homes every quarter to see if they were happy with the new service provided by our salespeople, follow the sales numbers to see if they were climbing and watch the gross margin to see if it was staying steady, increasing, or dropping. At first the sales staff resisted the plan but after a couple of months they started seeing the benefit for them and the company.

I had to develop a compensation system that did three things: reward the employee properly for their work, not hurt the company financially with that compensation plan and set up a community commission plan that would give a bonus to the sales group if they made quotas, help other staff reach their potential, and maintain the necessary gross margin.

The old system was commission on every new bed. A bed is defined as just that: the bed the patient sleeps in. If the home had six beds then the salesperson was able to get a commission of the sales from that bed. Each bed on average brought in 7 to 10 scripts and supplies, which ranged from $1,000 to $3,000 a month. If the salesperson sold larger items or large quantities of items like gloves, hospital beds, chairs or medical supplies then he or she received an extra bump in the commission. The problem here is that they would sell products to the homes well below the established gross margin that was set in the original training just to reach the total sales goals. Plus the salespeople felt that they were the most important part of the puzzle, and this caused the other parts of the team to build resentment up against them. Within the sales team they would not teach each other sales techniques that had worked for them because they wanted to be the top dog. The accounting department did not like it because the salespeople would make promises that were just not possible; for example, they would tell homes that they would get their bill on the first of the month, and we did not do them until the 25th of each month. As you can see the old system was not bad, but it had challenges, while the new system turned out to be the best thing that ever happened to me from a sales training aspect. The sale staff worked hand-in-hand with the in-house staff, which created a tension-free work zone, and the sales staff worked with each other to perfect their sales pitch and other techniques, which helped the company grow from $15,000 a month to $125,000 a month in six months.

One of the hardest things I had to do was to train the sales staff to identify the good, the bad and the ugly when it comes to a sale. The sales person's idea of a good sale is any large volume sale. My definition of a good sale is any size sale that maintains the gross profit margin. If fact if your sales people think that the larger the sale the better off they will be with no regard for the profit margin your business will soon be out of business.

An example of a bad sale (or in this case an almost bad sale) is when I sold Cedar Pharmacy. I had a medication-filling machine that cost $150,000 and when I sold Cedar to the buyer, they did not need it because they had a machine. I started to advertise the machine that we so happily named "FurrBee," and I was receiving tons of bites on the ad for lease and purchase. At first my mindset was to just get rid of it at any cost so I did not have to deal with it because it was really just dead money sitting in storage. But selling a piece of equipment, service or space at a huge discount just for the sake of "making money" is a mistake. You are thinking that you will make something that otherwise that would go to waste. You are creating a problem of selling a space, service, or equipment for less than it's worth, and I call this the accommodation trap.

It is called the *accommodation trap* because you are accommodating someone else's needs and not the needs of your business. Plus if you are just looking at the price and not the value of the space, equipment or service, then cutting your price will devalue your business. There are a few reasons why I will always avoid falling into the accommodation trap. First, there is a term cost of capital, and the cost of capital represents a handicap rate that a company must overcome before it can generate value. Meaning that if you are leasing or selling an unused item in your business for a low margin, then this is a waste of capital. Being an entrepreneur, money is limited to begin with, and if you continue to make bad decisions your company will be out of business. What if you have a regular customer that wants to use your services or space, and it is not available because you are letting a low margin customer use it? Again you are losing money, and this is bad for business. The last reason is because if you start selling or leasing your product, space or service at discounted prices, you are risking that the customers will find out and demand that they get a price break next time. Your margins have shrunk, all because your thought offering your products or services at a lower price was a good idea when times were slow. In my case I had four bids for my machine and I ended up taking the middle bid because I wanted to help out a friend starting his business, but I still made an acceptable profit.

    The ugly sale is when you do not listen to your customer's needs. I hate it when a salesperson walks into my place of business and tells me what I need and how I need it. Nothing will kill that sale faster, and I have been known to politely escort that person out of my business. Being a pharmacist I have to listen very carefully to what my patient needs before I can help them. Even when physicians call I have to listen very carefully to the diagnosis so I can recommend the proper pharmaceutical therapy for that patient. If you were reading carefully you would have read the keyword "*listen.*" The other side to listening is asking the right questions to see what they need to make their businesses better. On a rare occasion you may have a product or service that is head and shoulders above what the customer knows about and then after you listen you teach them about your new and innovative product or service. While you are in the sales meeting and you are actively listening to the customer, the next step is to ask questions that will make them evaluate why they may need a new product or service. You will need to ask about their needs, what needs to happen to improve their productivity and profits. Ask about the company's goals and then you will be ready to add value to that meeting and establish the type of experience that you want that customer to have with your company. Many salespeople feel that adding value is giving discounts or adding an extra piece to the puzzle. That is not value; that is a promotion. Adding value is giving something to the customer that they did not expect and you should give it often. The old saying was to "ask and you shall receive." The new saying is "give and you shall receive." I give free advice all the time to clients about business and offer free training and never ask for anything in return. When I do this for customers, they start to trust me. This trust builds a rapport with them through my social media or in person and they are ready to hire me and ask deeper questions about things in their business.

In the next chapter, I want to discuss how to act and perform like a $10 million CEO. I will give you some tips on how to plan your day and function with a purpose. I want to discuss the other research that I have done on what top CEOs do on a daily basis to keep themselves ready for the busy business day in front of them.

Chapter 10

Daily Focus Techniques

Have you ever walked into your office and did not know where to start? You look at two stacks of papers and don't know which one to start with? I remember after Cedar Pharmacy was getting busier and busier, my office work was getting more and more neglected. I had it in my mind that I needed to do everything. It was my business and if I was going to be successful then I had to handle the marketing, sales, inventory, customers and all the office work. Every now and then my wife Marisol would stop by to help out and pay some bills or reconcile QuickBooks. But, for the most part, everything was in my lap. Early on in my business, my accountant Troy was harping on me to get a bookkeeper. I did, but it took me awhile to learn. It wasn't that I did not want help; it was that I did not know I needed help.

It was a late Friday afternoon in September and I remember sitting at my desk thinking, *"What the hell is wrong with me?"* I used to be able to finish all my work and a little extra before the week's end. But as any entrepreneur can tell you, as time goes on in your business and you are becoming more successful, the workload seems to grow exponentially. Crazy how that works out! My next step was to really figure out a way to streamline my workload, because at this rate I would never leave the office and I would be a slave to my business. I started studying the top CEOs that I could find information on and the ones that I could talk to I would ask tons of questions. There were a ton of different things that each one did to reach their level of success, but the one thing I really wanted to know is, *How did they get everything done and still have time for family, friends, golf, the gym and any other hobbies?*

I am going to tease you a bit because I am only going to tell you about one of their secrets now. Let's get right to the number one thing that all the top CEOs like Bill Gates, David Marshall, Brendon Burchard, Jack Dorsey, Barack Obama and myself do to start our day. Not that I am a top CEO at a fortune 500 company or the president of a country but I am the CEO of my company and my staff and clients depend on me to do the right thing just like your company depends on you to do the right thing. The right thing is to plan your day out!

Jack Dorsey the founder of Twitter plans his week out in a theme method. Each weekday is dedicated to a specific area of his business. This is what his themed week looks like:

Monday: Management and running the company

Tuesday: Product

Wednesday: Marketing and communications, growth

Thursday: Developers and partnerships

Friday: Company culture and recruiting

The themed method helps Mr. Dorsey focus. Even being interrupted throughout his day, he can maintain the focus because of his thorough planning.

Barack Obama, the President of the United States, plans his mornings out by spending time eating breakfast with the family, takes his daughters to school and gets a workout in before he heads to the not just the office, but the Oval Office.

A key to making a schedule is to build some flexibility into the routine. If you have super strict schedule and you get interrupted you're not going to be flexible, then your day will be thrown for a loop. Kind of like driving a car with a flat tire.

What has helped me become an organized successful entrepreneur is that I write out my plan for the day. Don't just think, *Oh I will get this done and that done.* You need to write it down. I start the night before by writing down the top ten things that I want to do the next day. Now, these ten items don't always have to be new items.

Here is an example of my top ten list:

1. Read something related to my industry.

    a. You must always know what your competitors are doing!

2. Read something on business development.

    a. Learning should never stop! To master your craft you will always be a student.

3. Send two emails to touch base with JV partners or colleagues.

    a. When you launch a new product you will need JV partners to reach your goal.

  b. Colleagues because you never want to lose base with people you can bounce ideas around with.

4. Block time to send, answer, delete and file emails.

5. Check in with your staff to see how their days are going and what the progress is on their projects.

6. Take a break and talk with your employees, coworkers and partners about their personal life.

  a. Show you care about them, and they will care about the business.

7. Block time for the above projects.

  a. Lock the door, turn of the phone, and any other distracting things that can remove you from completing the project list.

8. Post five valuable pieces of content to social media.

  a. You must stay current with your customers.

9. Workout and Eat!

  a. Maintaining your health is a key to

CHAPTER 10 | DAILY FOCUS TECHNIQUES

your energy level to complete the tasks to be successful.

10. Take a few minutes to pat yourself on the back for the things that you have accomplished in your life.

The second part is that I write out three goals or projects that I need to get done for that day. With those three projects I write down the top five things that I need to get done for each goal or project and a list of the people that I need to get in touch with to ensure success with that project. It looks like this:

Projects

Project #1 The Must Happen List	Project #2 The Must Happen List	Project #3 The Must Happen List
1.	1.	1.
2.	2.	2.
3.	3.	3.
4.	4.	4.
5.	5.	5.

The Must-Happen List is the people and priorities that need to be completed **TODAY!**

Taking the 10-15 minutes every day to plan out the next day will help you reach a higher level of success in your life and business. I am living proof that being more organized and focused in my business life has made my personal life even better. I get to spend more time with Marisol and the boys or recharging my batteries – that means, I go play golf.

If you want to be more productive and have a successful business and personal life, then be focused on and committed to producing and progressing towards your goals. This will help you streamline your day-to-day routine, and if you need help to reach the goals then don't be like the early in my career and not ask for help. Go ask someone for his or her opinion on your situation. After talking with Harvey Mackay, the author of *Swim With the Sharks Without Being Eaten Alive* and CEO of a $500 million a year company, about how many coaches and consultants he has, I know that you can step outside your comfort zone and hire someone to help you pick up the slack so you can be more productive in your soon-to-be-successful business. By the way, he has over twenty coaches or consultants on his team.

I did not discuss the S.O.A.P Framework in this chapter, but the use of the S.O.A.P Framework was to increase your focus on your business. Establishing a new planning session

CHAPTER 10 | DAILY FOCUS TECHNIQUES

every morning or evening before you start the next day will allow your focus to be laser-sharp.

In the next chapter, I want to give you a quick overview of the S.O.A.P. Framework and give you some things to think about tomorrow when you get to your office with a daily plan in hand.

Chapter 11

Conclusion

Originally the S.O.A.P. Framework's purpose was to have a plan to put out fires in the business. But as time went on, I started to use and refine the S.O.A.P Framework to not only solve problems, but to review my systems to see if I could streamline them in any way to move the company closer to the $10 million a year goal. Using the S.O.A.P Framework, I was able to build key points with each section of my business and the businesses that I consulted for to help them grow and reach their goals. With the business plan, I learned that using it as a dynamic document helped to keep my focus on some of the more important things in the business like gross profit and watching the competition to make sure they did not get in front of me or start taking customers using my techniques. I now make a business plan that covers the entire business from A to Z and I also make a one-page dashboard business plan that

I use as a template to keep my focus on the growth of the business. In marketing I used the S.O.A.P Framework to identify the major flaws in my *hope marketing* strategy. Opening a business and not taking the time to market it to the right people at the right time is a waste of time. Using the S.O.A.P Framework in my marketing plan helped me focus my efforts on how to build trust and traffic for my business.

The other important thing is that it helped me identify my niche. I had to know what would make me different enough to get people in the door. I had to find a way to help make people's lives easier and more efficient with pharmacy than my competition. The biggest thing that happened to me in the marketing planning stage was that I was able to change my marketing funnel strategy and have it drip into the Customer Life Cycle. The change in my marketing focus was to continue to show the clients my services, products and information would be better than anywhere else.

With business strategies, I was able to utilize the S.O.A.P Framework to evaluate bad and good strategies. This tool changed my focus to adapt and alter the strategy to move in the direction of success and not failure. Another piece of the puzzle that every entrepreneur should know is that every part of the business has a strategic element to it. No matter how small that part of the business is, start on day one developing a system that explains the elements of that part of the business, so when the date comes to sell or pass it on, the new owner will be able to see how you did things in the business and why they were successful. The last thing you want is to sell your business and not have set successful systems in place and then watch the business fail. Those kinds of things damage your legacy.

In the vendor and inventory chapter, the lesson learned was to focus your efforts on building relationships with your vendors. In any new business the last thing you want to waste money if you don't need to. As a matter a fact you really don't want to waste money at any point in your business, it is crucial that your clarity is razor-sharp when you are signing a new vendor, changing or renewing a contract with a vendor, purchasing or selling a piece or all of the business. Being able to carefully build a process to evaluate how vendors are chosen and contracts are signed will go a long way to building a bigger and better business.

Knowing your numbers, what they mean and how to follow them gives a clear and concise view of your business. The objective measure of the finances gives a snapshot of the company at any point in time. Remember not to fall in to the trap of the accountant and only looking at the numbers from the historical point only. Remember you are an entrepreneur and risk is in your blood. Look at the numbers to figure out where you are and what you need to do to get to the next goal or level of success you want to achieve.

      Using the S.O.A.P Framework to clear up the meaning of sales and the importance of keeping the sales people working within the gross margin numbers is the focal point that needs to be hammered home every day in business. Selling stuff is great but if the bills are not getting paid and your employees are not happy with the systems set in place then failure is and will be lurking around the corner to take the business down. By taking the time to establish clear and concise sales goals, techniques, and gross margin limits allowed the sales people to thrive. The S.O.A.P Framework helped me identify a new way of paying the sales staff so they would work better as a team and with the inside staff. By changing my focus from big numbers to numbers that made sense and the being able to teach this to the staff was a turning point in the pharmacy. This strategy helped increase the sales numbers 59% in three months. That is one section of the sales that truly helped me turn the page so then I could take the time to focus on other parts of the business. I knew that selling the business in three to five years was my main goal. With this goal in mind I had to move quickly and take risk that was calculated, but not to the point an attorney would calculate risk because they suck the risk out. I say this not because I dislike my attorney and life long friend Mr. Touchstone, but he is so conservative compared to business entrepreneurs.

Being able to organize yourself on a day-to-day basis is one of the major keys to success. By reviewing what some of the top business minds of our time do with their time has inspired me to change the way I conduct business. If you have not heard the quote "organization is the key to success," it is truer today than ever before. What I mean is that with all the distractions that you have in your life, from a spouse, kids, work, cell phone, social media, emails and the list goes on but I am sure you get my drift. Take the time to write down the *Ten Things To Do List* and the three projects list and try it for five weeks. I promise that you will get better results from your life and your business by taking the ten minutes to organize your day.

Chapter 11 | Conclusion

The first thing I want you to do after reading this book is run, don't walk, back to your business and start evaluating every division of the business. Look at it with a keen eye and apply the S.O.A.P. Framework to each part to see if there might be a better way of doing it. I would have never changed some of my strategies if I had not used S.O.A.P. Framework. The example that stands out is changing the sales people from commission to salary with bonus. By taking this time to reevaluate the business, it will bring you back to that intimate level that you experienced in the beginning of the business. This is just what your family and your business will need to get to the next level.

I want to tell you one last story of one of my clients. She was a beautiful young girl with tons of ambition and drive when I met her. She had her life plan all ready to go and a basic plan for her career. She came from a family that is not big on college graduates and entrepreneurs, but somehow she stepped out of the darkness and into the light. She was finishing school at UCSD and wanted to go to law school. So she went and got a job at a local law firm here in San Diego and soon realized that this was not the career path for her. She figured out a new plan and leaving the law school path would be good for her because it was not her passion. I am a firm believer in doing things that you are passionate about because your chances of success are higher.

After talking, one of the things that she was passionate about was interior design. The next day she found a design school that she liked, and off she went happy as a clam to learn the world of design. Over the next three years, learning and applying the skills she was learning in design school was just a Band-Aid to what her real passion was and is still today. Unfortunately it was not that easy for her to see what her passion real was at that time, and over the next couple of years she went through two more career changes as well as being a mom to her two boys. Then finally a friend of hers introduced her to running and group workouts, and the love affair with working out began. Over the next year, she went from an active mom that was not happy with her career or life to a super workout maniac and someone that had a full transformation in her life. Now that she is in the best shape of her life, she calls me and we sit down again to figure how she can turn her love of fitness into a career. Since that conversation she started a blog about food, fitness, and motivation, started training clients and shooting free workout videos and posting them on YouTube. When we worked on her other projects or careers I could feel that the passion was not there. I am sure that we have all done things that we felt we had to but were not really happy do them. Her focus and determination has lead to some amazing advances in her career. She gets up every day at five a.m. to train her clients and shoot videos, or post blogs to motivate the people around the world to get up and move. Working together she is starting to build a career in fitness and, most importantly, she is building a career that she loves and it shows. The entrepreneurial spirit in her is alive and well and it just goes to show you that you can be knocked down and kicked a couple thousand times, but you and only you, have the power to change your life so that you can make a positive impact on the lives that you touch. Our world needs more people like this girl, not only for the positive attitude, but she is living proof that entrepreneurs are resilient and Marisol Fitness is the proof. This girl is one of the major reasons why I am where I am at today and I owe her a debt of gratitude for her love, trust and compassion. Her name is Marisol and she is my wife and the mother of my awesome boys, Liam and Bryce. The best part is that she is changing the lives of men and women every day in helping them realize that they can be fit and happy with what they see in the mirror daily. The focus and resiliency that Marisol has is the whole meaning of this book and why I developed the S.O.A.P. Framework.

Now, take the time. Today is the day to take your business to the next level and *focus* on the dreams and goals that you have for yourself and your family. In doing so, your business can be the beacon of hope that helps others live an easier life. Live positively, share your message and let your business make a difference.

About The Author

Bernard Gramlich is the creator of the S.O.A.P. Framework and the founder of Dr. Gram Consulting. After being a serial entrepreneur for over 35 years, he now helps businesses enhance their problem solving skills while streamlining their processes so they can become more efficient and productive without suffering through lost sales, bad employees, and lackluster profits like he experienced in the beginning of his entrepreneurial ventures.

His love for business started at the ripe age of 10 when he took over his mother's Amway account and grew it into diamond status. Since then, he has been hooked on learning and growing more efficient businesses. Those early business failures and successes have paved the way for his now thriving consulting business. Dr. Gramlich has owned or co-owned 12 businesses throughout his career and each one has taught him valuable lessons of growth he was able to apply to each new venture.

Now, he dedicates his time to teaching managers, business owners and entrepreneurs his coveted techniques for business success through his website, **www.drgramconsulting.com**.

Dr. Gramlich graduated from USC with his bachelor's degree and went on to receive his doctoral degree in Pharmacy from Western University of Health Sciences. He received his Street MBA from working hard and learning from his failures and successes. He believes learning is a lifelong process that leads to a road of growth and success. He also believes everyone has a message or lesson to teach whether it is your family, clients, and even strangers on the street.

Printed in Great Britain
by Amazon